# A Practical Guide to Employee Share Schemes

# A Practical Guide to Employee Share Schemes

Nitzan Cohen LLB (Hons)
NC Tax Consultancy

Law Brief Publishing

Published 2019 by Law Brief Publishing, an imprint of Law Brief Publishing Ltd
30 The Parks
Minehead
Somerset
TA24 8BT

www.lawbriefpublishing.com

Paperback: 978-1-912687-46-6

*This book is dedicated to my parents for their continuing help and support and for the fact that, without them, this book would never have been written. It is also dedicated to those of you who have been there for me along my legal career.*

# PREFACE

Share and option schemes have been around for quite some time now. However, the uptake has, at times, been slow and can definitely get better. This book has been written as a practical guide to lawyers, accountants and other professionals. It is also aimed at business owners, company directors and senior employees.

The use and introduction of share and option schemes into UK businesses have been proved to greatly assist in the recruitment and continuing incentivisation of key employees in private and public companies. Share schemes are also used to reward employees for their efforts and, where possible, with good tax reliefs and benefits to companies and their employees.

It is written as a practical guide so that readers can gain a basic understanding of the available schemes and their tax implications. Readers should be able to gauge the type of scheme that may be available to their clients' or to their own businesses together with the potential benefits to companies and their employees. An attempt has been made to avoid legalese and too many references to statute and case law so that readers can read through it in order to benefit from the whole story that is share and option schemes.

This first edition of the book states the law as it is on 31st August 2019.

Nitzan Cohen
October 2019

# CONTENTS

# CHAPTER ONE
# BACKGROUND

*What is a share scheme or option scheme?*

Before we can answer this question, we need to understand the problem or issue that it is meant to solve.

Share or option schemes are mainly relevant to companies that can issue shares to individuals and other legal persons. In a typical limited liability private company, the shareholders own the company but may not run the company in terms of day to day dealings with employees, customers and other third-party providers. They may not, other than in relation to specific important decision relating to the company, get involved in the general decision making relating to the business of the company.

Now let us start with a basic understanding of what companies do in order to grow their business. In order to grow a business, a company needs, amongst other things, to consider taking advantage of one of the most important assets that it has – people.

A company may be set up by a number of individuals who, together, have an idea for a business. Those individuals may indeed have a good idea but may struggle to translate that idea into a thriving business. They may not be 'business savvy' and will definitely need to consider employing the right people to do just that – convert the idea into a business. For example, a carpenter or cabinet maker may produce good quality products and receive very good feedback from customers. Whilst he may be a very good tradesman, he may not be a very good businessman in terms of operating and growing a business, as it requires more than carpentry skills. He may possess the required skills but help is, mostly, needed.

So, to take care of the business side, the company will employ directors to run its business. The original shareholders or founders of the company may start by running the company themselves as directors and may even go on acting as directors for as long as they own the company. However, in some cases the founders may employ the 'right' people for the job of running the company depending on the type of business and the required skill etc.

The directors, therefore, may or may not be shareholders in the company. The directors of the company will, obviously, expect to be rewarded for their services to the company. They will, normally, receive a salary from the company and other benefits under a service contract but given their potential valuable contribution to the company, they may wish to have a stake or a share in the company so that their 'true worth' to the company is appreciated by way of participation in any future growth in the company, which, to a large extent, is down to them. Indeed, the company may also wish to reward them in that way in order to ensure that they stay with the company and don't seek alternative employment with a competitor or simply start a new business in competition with the company.

The company may also employ some individuals who may be experts in their field and as far as the company is concerned, such individuals may be key employees and essential to the success of the company. Such individuals may not be directors in the company. Their expectation in participating in the company's future success may be similar to that of the current directors of the company.

Having said that, it is very important to remember that participation in the ownership of a private company does not necessarily mean that the future of the owners of the company is certain in terms of the expected financial reward. It is a risky form of investment, as the value of shares can go down as well as up and so the participators' or shareholders' investment in the company. However, for those involved in the company, they may consider it a risk worth taking, as they ought to believe in their own abilities to drive the business of the company forward so that they can build a successful business resulting in all of them being rewarded in the future.

An equity stake in the form of share ownership in the company is, therefore, arguably inevitable. In order to incentivise, retain and recruit existing or new directors and other key employees (as the case may be), the company will need to consider this as part of its overall business structure and plan. Equity stake in the company is usually expected and nowadays forms part of the remuneration package of key employees. It helps in the recruitment process when money is tight and salary payments and other benefits do not reflect the true value received from those individuals.

It also helps in aligning the expectation of shareholders with that of directors and key employees by ensuring that directors and key employees see the business as a form of investment from which they derive a direct benefit rather than a potential temporary job from which to receive a salary until a better job comes along with better financial rewards.

Beyond the personal expectation of existing shareholders and key employees, the government is encouraging the investment by employees in the form of participation in the ownership of private companies (and to some extent, listed companies) as, it believes, such participation will help companies grow and be more profitable. In turn, those companies will employ and retain more employees. As far as the wider national economy is concerned, the overall growth in terms of the number of people employed, means more taxes paid to the government and less benefits paid to those who are able but do not form part of the job market, allowing more investments by the government on infrastructure and other national interests.

The original shareholders of the company will need to consider their future planning at the early stages of setting up. However, they don't always do perhaps because they are not aware of the future prospects of the company and in most cases such issues become relevant when the company is established for a number of years but is considering an expansion that requires the employing of new talents.

The shareholders may wish to consider issuing shares to directors and key employees in order to ensure that they are sufficiently incentivised to help grow the business of the company. When the company is at its start-up stage, this is less of a problem. The value of the shares in the company is relatively minimal so new joiners are more likely to afford to buy into the ownership club. However, it is more complicated when it is considered by shareholders of an established company. The share value may be high and any stake in the company may be expensive even for a very small stake. Affordability may, therefore, be an issue for new joiners.

The company cannot simply give shares for free without triggering various tax implications to both the individuals and the company itself, which by itself may be an expensive option for the parties.

Whilst affordability is an issue and, at times, a major one, the parties do not necessarily want to abandon the idea of share ownership in the company.

*So, what can they do?*

In a nutshell, the options are:

- Issue shares to directors and key employees in return for a payment that represents market value for the shares in the company. Under this option, the cost to the individuals is the amount paid for the shares;

- Shares are gifted to the employees as a form of benefit, either outright or by way of a reduction in the market value of the shares, but subject to the payment by the company and the individuals of income tax and, potentially, national insurance contributions (whether or not national insurance contributions are payable is discussed later in the book) on the full amount of the benefit. Here, the cost to the individuals is whatever amount they pay for the shares in the company plus any income tax and national insurance contributions, if any, on the value of the benefit that they receive from the company.

Now that we've established that cost and affordability is possibly the main issue or, to some extent, problem to any new joiners, we can consider other issues that may create barriers to the sought-after equity stake in the company.

Existing shareholders may not feel comfortable with the idea that new directors or other key employees receive equity stake in the company before delivering value and effectively proving their worth to the company. Whilst shares can be bought back in certain circumstances where the key employee does not act in a way that is expected of him or her and for the same amount that the employee has paid for the shares, the process can be avoided by issuing shares at a later stage.

Shareholders may also feel uncomfortable with the idea of sharing sensitive and other confidential information with new shareholders. They may not want them to have the ability to vote or even receive dividends if the intention is for them to simply benefit from a future growth in the company's capital value perhaps on the eventual sale of the company or on the happening of other major events such as listing of the company on the stock market or a sale of the company's business. Such concerns can, to some extent, be resolved by creating a different class of shares with enhanced restrictions on the ability of key employees to vote, receive dividends and so on.

In order to solve that affordability issue and other issues referred to above, we can now delve into the world of share or option schemes under which employees receive or acquire shares in the company or an option to receive or acquire shares in the company immediately or at a later date in a way that protects the interests of existing shareholders but, most importantly, at a more affordable value to directors and key employees and in a tax efficient way, where possible.

However, just before we go into it, we will look into various concepts that will assist us in understanding the tax and other legal implications that are relevant to share and option schemes.

And something to bear in mind that, whilst a particular emphasis is made in relation to directors and key employees in a company, it is very important to note that the issues referred to above and later in the book are not limited to them but are relevant to all employees of the company. Investors who are not employees of the company are not affected and do not have the same limitations that employees have as, the tax implications, that are of concern, of share acquisitions in a company is only relevant to those individuals who acquire shares by reason of their employment with the company.

# CHAPTER TWO
# READILY CONVERTIBLE ASSETS (RCAS)

Whenever employees or directors of a company acquire or propose to acquire shares in the company in which they are employed or in another company within the same group of companies by reason of their employment with the company or the group, it is very important to consider and be mindful of the tax implications that may arise on any benefit received by them. Any benefit received on acquisition is normally subject to income tax and in some cases, national insurance contributions. Any implications that may give rise to a liability under the inheritance tax legislation is outside the scope of this book but should be considered in addition to other taxes that may apply to the acquisition.

Income tax comes in many different forms but essentially it is tax on the personal employment income of an individual. When a benefit, other than cash, is received by an employee by reason of that employee's employment in the company, the benefit received by that employee is also subject to income tax but under a different piece of legislation or more like – pieces – a few. In the case of a benefit, other than cash, the value of the benefit will need to be valued and quantified so that the correct liability to income tax is assessed. Later on, we will consider some of the different forms of income tax and the way that they interact with share and option schemes.

Capital gains tax is payable on the amount of the gain that is realised from the sale of a capital asset.

*How do you know if the asset is a capital one?*

Well, in a simple way, one can recognise a capital asset because it is acquired or held with the intention that, whilst it may provide the owner of the capital assets with income during the period of ownership, it appreciates in value over time and is normally acquired as a long-term investment. Shares in a company are, normally, capital assets, any gain realised from the sale of those shares will be subject to capital gains tax. It is therefore tax on the disposal of a capital asset. Capital gains tax goes beyond a disposal as we know it and can even be relevant when any gain is realised from a capital asset where, for example, the asset is destroyed or gifted but this is not relevant in the context of share or option schemes so for the moment can be left at that.

A capital item can be subject to both income tax and capital gains tax. Income tax on acquisition and throughout the period of ownership and capital gains tax on the disposal of the capital asset.

Now that we've touched very briefly, well for the moment, on what is income tax and capital gains tax, this chapter is, actually, all about national insurance contributions.

In the context of earnings from employment, which is defined to include any remuneration or profit derived from an employment, an employer is under an obligation under the Pay As You Earn (PAYE) system, amongst other things, to:

- Deduct income tax from any earnings from employment of an employee;
- Deduct Class 1 employee's national insurance contributions; and
- Account to HMRC for the amounts so deducted and also pay to HMRC Class 1 employer's national insurance contributions on the amount of income tax deducted.

The obligation to deduct primary (employee) Class 1 and secondary (employer) national insurance contributions (NICs) normally follows that of income tax so to the extent income tax is required to be deducted under PAYE, NICs will also be required to be deducted and accounted to HMRC by the employer.

If the employer is not required to deduct income tax from the employee's earnings, the employee will be required to account to HMRC for the income tax by completing a self-assessment tax return. NICs will not normally be payable by the employee or employer on that income. Any amounts deducted under PAYE must be paid to HMRC by the employer relatively quickly after the deduction is made whereas, if the employee is required to complete a self-assessment return in respect of any amount of income tax, the return and payment of the tax due will need to be made by the 31 of January after the end of the relevant tax year in which the liability arises.

*Will the employer be required to operate PAYE in any event?*

Consider a normal situation under which an employee is entitled to a salary in respect of the employee's employment. The employer pays it in cash directly to the employee's bank account. The employer will always be required to operate the PAYE system in relation to any such cash payments to the employee.

However, what if an employee receives various benefits that are not cash? For example, an employee may be entitled to exercise an option to acquire shares in the company or indeed may receive shares in the company as a gift or for a price that represents a discount to the market value or, in other words, the employee acquires the shares at an undervalue. The payment for the shares on exercise may not represent market value. A benefit is, seemingly, received by the employee on which, potentially, income tax is due.

Broadly speaking, if and to the extent any benefit that the employee receives from the employer is not subject to income tax, NICs will not be payable on that benefit. If income tax is payable in respect of an asset received by the employee such as shares, then, in the context of shares or any other non-cash assets, NICs will also be payable on that benefit if the shares or non-cash assets are readily convertible assets or RCAs.

So, to summarise:

- Earnings from employment that are received by an employee in cash or in the form of RCAs will always be subject to the operation of PAYE by the employer resulting in the employer having to deduct income tax and NICs from the earnings of the employee and account to HMRC for the amounts so deducted;

- Any employment income received by an employee in the form of assets that are not RCAs will not be subject to the PAYE system. The employee will be required to pay income tax under self-assessment and no NICs liabilities will arise.

*What are RCAs?*

As a starting point we need to establish what is an asset. It may seem quite obvious and, in most cases, it is probably just that. However, section 701 of Income Tax (Earnings and Pensions) Act 2003 (ITEPA 2003) defines the term 'Asset' to include "any property, and in particular, any investment of a kind specified in Part 3 of the Financial Services and Markets Act 2000 (Regulated Activities) Order 2001 (SI2001/544)".

Section 701 also refers to a number of items that are not included within the term 'Asset'. A couple of them relate to two approved schemes (Save As You Earn and Company Share Option Plan) but are quite limited in scope so whilst important to note, may only become relevant in very limited circumstances.

Assets that are always RCAs

As the name suggests, the overall idea is that the asset can be relatively and easily converted into cash. However, to make life a bit easier, section 702 of ITEPA 2003 provides a list of assets that are always RCAs so that any employment income arising from such assets will always be subject to the operation of PAYE.

These are:

- An asset capable of being sold or otherwise realised on a recognised investment exchange (within the meaning of the Financial Services and Markets Act 2000), the London Bullion Market, the New York Stock Exchange, or a market for the time being specified in PAYE regulations;

- An asset consisting in the rights of an assignee, or any other rights, in respect of a money debt that is or may become due to the employer or any other person; property that is subject to a warehousing regime, or any right in respect of property so subject; or anything that is likely (without anything being done by the employee) to give rise to, or to become, a right enabling a person to obtain an amount or total amount of money which is likely to be similar to the expense incurred in the provision of the asset;

- An asset for which trading arrangements are in existence, or are likely to come into existence in accordance with any arrangements of another description existing when the asset is provided, or any understanding existing at that time;

- An asset consisting in securities which is not a readily convertible asset apart from this subsection is to be treated as a readily convertible asset unless the securities are shares that are corporation tax deductible.

As always, no definition is ever perfect. However, in regard to assets for which trading arrangements exist and securities that are shares that are not deductible for corporation tax purposes so, effectively, any income tax arising in respect of those assets will be subject to the operation of the PAYE system, it is important to note, more particularly, in the context of share schemes:

- Many schemes are exercised on a sale of a company. At that time trading arrangements exist in relation to the shares, the subject matter of the option. Having said that, it is not always so simple to determine whether trading arrangements exist.

The courts have considered the concept in cases where assets have been transferred to employees but in circumstances where no obvious sale or transfer to a third party exists;

- The existence of an employee benefit trust (EBT) in the company creates an internal market within the company enabling employees to acquire and sale shares within the company. Trading arrangements, therefore, exist in relation to such shares;

- Any transaction in shares where the company is not entitled to a corporation tax deduction in relation to such shares will be RCAs. Consequently, shares that are not fully paid-up, redeemable shares or other shares that do not form part of the ordinary share capital of the company will always be RCAs.

*Why is it important?*

When considering the setting up of an approved or tax advantaged share scheme on behalf of a company, the parties to the scheme will expect any benefits to be free from income tax and NICs. When the scheme is unapproved or non-tax advantaged, income tax may or may not be payable on any benefit received. There are circumstances under which the exercise of options or the acquisition of shares pursuant to a share scheme, may give rise to an income tax liability (this will be considered further later in relation to each of the schemes). The company will need to consider how to deal with that liability by reference to the following:

- If the PAYE system applies:

  - the PAYE system must be operated by the employer (and not by the person setting-up or operating the scheme if different from the employer company). It involves the assessment by the employer company of the amount of income tax to be deducted from the employee together with primary Class 1 NICs. The employer will need to pay to HMRC the amount so deducted together with the secondary Class 1 NICs;

- ○ the employer is normally required to pay to HMRC the amounts deducted from employees on a monthly basis;

- ○ amounts in respect of income tax and NICs may be required to be deducted at a time when the relevant employee is no longer an employee of the company. The company will need to consider its ability to recover such amounts from that employee by way of an indemnity or otherwise.

- If the PAYE system does not apply:

  - ○ the obligation to settle the income tax liability is that of the employee by the employee completing a self-assessment tax return. Any failure to notify HMRC or pay the income tax due will result in interest and penalties being imposed on the employee not the employer company;

  - ○ the tax return will need to be filed and the income tax paid by the employee by the 31 of January after the end of the relevant tax year. No NICs is payable by either the employee or the employer in relation to that payment;

  - ○ as the employer company is not responsible to operate the PAYE system in relation to the income tax liability of the employee, it will not need to concern itself with any future recovery action on non-payment by the employee.

# CHAPTER THREE
# ENTREPRENEURS' RELIEF (ER)

ER is a very important relief to consider and companies will need to make sure that, as far as possible, the conditions for the relief are considered in good time so that the ability to claim the relief is not jeopardised simply because the company or the relevant employee negligently fails to consider it in advance resulting in any of them failing to ultimately comply with any of the relevant conditions for the relief.

If any of the conditions for the relief are not complied with by both the company and the individual then the relief will not be available and the individual will have to pay CGT on any gain realised from the sale of the shares in the company at the current rate (or the prevailing rate at the relevant time) of 20% rather than the reduced rate of 10% after a successful claim is made for ER.

*What is ER?*

ER is a relief that reduces the rate of capital gains tax (CGT) payable by individuals on a disposal of qualifying business assets.

Capital gains on disposal of shares are now taxed at 10% (basic rate taxpayers) and 20% (higher rate taxpayers). If ER applies, capital gains tax is reduced to 10% in respect of the amount of any qualifying capital gains not exceeding £10 million. The current lifetime limit of £10 million applies to disposals which have occurred in the period from 6 April 2011.

The relief was introduced in 2008 with a lifetime limit of £1 million. The lifetime limit was then doubled to £2 million with effect from 6 April 2010 and then increased again to £5 million for disposals occurring on or after 23 June 2010. Any claim in previous periods under the previous lifetime limits counts towards the current lifetime limit of £10 million.

Any gain that exceeds that amount will be subject to CGT at the full rate that applies to that gain. For example, if shares are sold for £20 million and the gain on that disposal is £18 million, then, subject to other reliefs and allowances that may apply to that disposal, the relevant individual may claim ER in respect of the first £10 million at the rate of 10% and the balance will be subject to CGT at the full rate of 20%. In that case, the individual has exhausted the lifetime limit of £10 million so any future disposal of a qualifying business asset will not qualify for the relief. Any amount not claimed up to the lifetime limit of £10 million can be claimed on any future disposal of qualifying business assets.

The relief is not automatic and must be claimed on or before the first anniversary of the 31 January after the end of the tax year of disposal. For example, if a disposal of shares occurs in the tax year 2018/2019, a claim for ER can be made by 31 January 2021. The relief is claimed by the individual by completing his or her self-assessment tax return for the relevant period.

The term 'lifetime' could be confusing. ER replaced the old taper relief. It is not uncommon for various reliefs and allowances to be withdrawn, replaced or generally amended. It is important to bear in mind that, whilst it is termed as a lifetime limit, it may no longer be available after the next budget or in the next few years. If one is entitled to claim the relief then one ought to claim it and don't leave it for a future disposal on the basis that it is there for life as it may no longer be available.

*What is a qualifying capital gain?*

Not all capital gains qualify for ER. As far as shares are concerned, the relevant individual disposing of shares in the company needs to ensure that the gain on disposal is, indeed, a capital gain and is not reclassified by HMRC as an income of that individual due to the application of any relevant anti-avoidance provision and therefore subject to income tax at the relevant income tax rates which, at current rates, are higher than the CGT rates.

Otherwise, before the individual can claim ER in respect of disposal of shares in the company, all of the following conditions must be satisfied throughout the period of 24 months (with effect from 6 April 2019 the period has been extended to 24 months. The period was 12 months before that date) ending with the date of disposal:

- The company is a trading company or the holding company of a trading group;
- The individual holds at least 5% of the issued share capital in the company allowing him or her to exercise at least 5% of the voting rights in that company. With effect from 29 October 2018, the individual must, in addition to having a 5% voting rights, be beneficially entitled to 5% of any distributable profits available to shareholders on a winding up of the company or on a sale of that company;
- The individual is an employee or officer of the company (whether full or part time) or any other company that is a member of a trading group.

Important points to note in connection with the above conditions:

The Company:

The company must be a trading company or the holding company of a trading group. A group is defined to include the holding company and its 51% subsidiaries. 51% means that more than half of the ordinary share capital of the subsidiary is directly or indirectly owned by another company.

Whether or not the relevant company or group is a trading company, for the purpose of ER, may not be so easy to ascertain. On the face of it, one may assume that the company is a trading company on the basis that it is involved in what is generally understood to be a trade. However, legislation defines a trading company as a company that carries on trading activities and does not carry on other non-trading activities to a substantial extent. The same applies to a trading group so that, looking at the activities of the group as a whole, the non-trading activities of the group must not be substantial.

*What is the meaning of substantial?*

In order to clarify the position so that it is not open to too many arguments about what is substantial, HMRC have confirmed their interpretation of the phrase 'substantial extent' to mean more than 20%. So effectively, if a trading company's non-trading activities amount to more than 20%, that company, whilst a trading company in the eyes of its founders and shareholders, may not be classified as a trading company for the purpose of ER.

*How can we measure non-trading activities?*

This is the point where it potentially gets complicated. We know the non-trading activities must not exceed 20% but by reference to what? Are we going to measure those activities by reference to the company's gross profits? Gross assets value? And the activity itself, how can we assess whether it is a trading activity or a non-trading activity?

In assessing activities of the company, HMRC will be looking at various indicators, each on its own may serve as a clear indication that the company is not a trading company for the purpose of ER. In some cases, more than one indicator may be needed in order to assess the situation. It is ultimately a question of fact which will be based on the circumstances that are relevant to each company.

Some indicators to be considered whereby the company may not be a trading company include:

- The company's income receipts from non-trading activities as opposed to trading activities. If income receipts from non-trading activities exceed that of the company's trading activities, the company may not be trading;

- The company may have a large portfolio of non-trading assets such as office blocks that it keeps as an investment. If that portfolio exceeds the trading asset base of the company, the company may, again, not be a trading company;

- If the company's directors devote a substantial part of their time to managing non-business activities or assets of the company, this, by itself, may be an indication that the company's non-trading activities are substantial.

However, the above indicators may need to be looked at along with other indicators that may be relevant to the company, the company's history, the way it conducts its business etc. in which case the final determination may be reversed so that the company is classified as a trading company. Compare the above with the following:

- A company has generated large amount of cash and is proposing to expand its trading business. For a while, the cash has been invested until such time that an expansion is possible. The holding of cash will not prevent the company from being classified as a trading company;

- A company may require an office building or factory for the purpose of its trading activities. The acquisition of what seems to be an investment asset may not jeopardise the company's trading status.

The employee or officer of the company:

Provided that all the conditions referred to above are satisfied so that the relevant individual is able to validly claim the relief on any gain arising on disposal of shares or other securities, any additional shares acquired by that individual over the 5% holding will also qualify for the relief even if the additional shares have been held for less than the requisite period. However, if the individual holds less than 5% of the ordinary share capital, the two years period is not relevant and is not counted until the 5% holding is achieved. Therefore, the date of acquisition of any additional shares, which, for the first-time results in the holding of shares being equal to, or exceeding the qualifying 5% holding, will start the clock on the two years period.

Jointly owned shares may result in the relief not applying on disposal of those shares. This is because, for CGT purposes, each of the joint owners is treated as having an equal proportion of the shares and each is entitled to claim the relief separately from the other. Consider the following, not so uncommon situation, whereby a husband and wife together own 6% of the ordinary share capital in the company. For the purpose of the example we can assume that all other conditions are satisfied for the relief to apply. However, as each of them is treated as owning 3% of the ordinary share capital in the company, the relief will not apply. In order to secure the availability of the relief in such circumstances one of the joint owners will need to transfer his or her shares to the other joint owner. Once the relevant conditions have been satisfied in relation to the shares (more particularly, the period of ownership after such transfer) the relief may be available.

With effect from 6 April 2013 but in relation to shares acquired on or after 5 April 2012, and only in relation to the Enterprise Management Incentive Scheme (EMI Scheme):

- The 5% requirement is relaxed on disposal of any shares acquired following an exercise of EMI options so, effectively, they can benefit from the relief even if their holding of shares on exercise is less than 5%;

- The two years requirement includes the period in which the EMI option was held. So, effectively, if an individual holds an EMI option for a period of, at least, two years and then that individual exercises the options, on, say, a sale of the company to a third party, by acquiring shares in the company for a very short period of time, as that individual will be required to sell the shares along with the other shareholders, the period of holding of the EMI option is aggregated with the holding period of shares. If the combined period of holding, immediately before disposal of the shares, exceeds two years, then the two years requirement will have been satisfied in relation to that individual.

However, given that the favourable treatment is limited to shares acquired under the EMI Scheme and cannot be extended to any other shares in the company, any other shares held by that individual (not under an EMI Scheme) will be subject to all the qualifying conditions for the relief to apply.

The combination of the above conditions for the individual to hold 5% of the ordinary share capital and be employee of the company immediately before disposal means that on a disposal of shares in the company, the individual must be an officer or employee of the company at that time.

It is not unusual, when a dispute arises within a company, for officers or employees who are also shareholders in the company to resign and then commence negotiations for the sale of their shares in the company whether by way of a share buyback by the company directly from the relevant individual, to an employee benefit trust or to another shareholder in the company. In such circumstances, the individual will lose his or her right to claim ER on the basis that the relevant individual is no longer an officer or employee of the company on the date of disposal of the shares. It is therefore important to remain an officer or employee of the company until the shares are sold by that individual.

# CHAPTER FOUR
# EMPLOYMENT RELATED SECURITIES – RESTRICTED SECURITIES

The restricted securities regime was introduced with effect from 16 April 2003. It applies to any shares or securities acquired from that date so any shares or securities acquired before 16 April 2003 will not be subject to the regime described below.

The regime is relevant to any securities received or acquired by reason of employment. This means that any securities received or acquired by employees will be subject to the regime if they are restricted. However, securities may also be acquired by others by reason of their connection with the employee so provided that they receive any benefit by reason of the employee's employment in the company, such securities will also be restricted securities and subject to the regime even if the holder in question is not an employee of the company.

For convenience, the remainder of this chapter will consider shares as securities rather than any other type of securities.

The restricted securities regime was introduced in order to impose an income tax charge on the difference between the actual or restricted market value and the unrestricted market value of shares acquired or received by an employee (this is on the basis that the employee acquiring the shares pays the actual market value).

The restricted securities regime is not looking to tax the employee at the point of acquisition unless the employee elects for any untaxed amount to be subject to income tax at that point. Otherwise, the income tax charge is imposed at the time when any restrictions on the shares are lifted either by way of sale of those securities or by simply removing any restrictions on them.

Sounds complicated! So, before we look at what this regime is all about let us go back in time to before 16 April 2013.

By way of background and in order to better understand what the restricted securities regime is trying to achieve, the following example will illustrate why it was needed by looking at the taxing position before the introduction of the regime.

Let us look at Joanna, an employee in ABC Limited. In 2002 she acquired shares in the company. She paid a reduced amount on the basis that the shares were heavily restricted (more on this a bit later). The reduced amount was not considered a sale to Joanna at undervalue because the price paid by Joanna reflected the true value of the shares when she acquired them, as they were heavily restricted. In other words, Joanna paid the actual market value for the shares. So far so good.

Few years later, an unconnected third-party buyer is found for ABC Limited. Any restrictions attaching to the shares are lifted at that time and effectively ignored on the basis that the buyer is agreeing to pay the full unrestricted market value of the company. The buyer is not interested in any restrictions which, at the time of sale are attached to the shares. The buyer will most probably draft new articles of association and perhaps introduce new restrictions on the shares.

However, Joanna is entitled to a consideration, or an amount for the sale of her shares, that reflects her percentage holding in the company. No account is taken for the fact that her shares are now as valuable as any other shares in the company simply by reason of the removal of the restrictions. Whilst Joanna originally acquired the shares for a relatively small amount due to the restrictions, on disposal of the shares to a third-party, that reduction or the price difference between what Joanna paid for her shares and the unrestricted market value of those shares now seems more like a form of an employment benefit on which no tax is paid.

The restricted securities regime has been introduced in order to change that situation so now an income tax charge is imposed on the benefit received by the employee when the restrictions are lifted or otherwise removed.

The regime considers two different values for the shares in a company:

- One is the Actual Market Value (AMV) or Restricted Market Value (RMV) – this is the value of the shares subject to restrictions. As they are less valuable than other shares in the company, they have a value that reflects that true value to the employee;

- The other value is the Unrestricted Market Value (UMV) – this value ignores any restrictions attaching to the shares. In other words, this value reflects what a third-party may agree to pay for the shares in the company.

*What restrictions fall within the regime?*

The following three categories are the type of restrictions that are relevant to the restricted securities regime:

- Forfeiture restriction. Under this restriction, the employee may be required to transfer his or her shares if certain circumstances arise or do not arise. For example, on leaving employment the employee may be required to sell his or her shares at less than the full unrestricted market value;

- Limitation restriction. Under this restriction, the employee's freedom to dispose of his or her shares or proceeds of their sale may be restricted. For example, the employee's shares may be subject to restrictions on transfer or where the employee agrees to waive voting or dividend rights; and

- Disadvantage restriction is a more general restriction that reflects any disadvantage suffered by the employee. It is meant to cover any form of disadvantage that is not covered by the other two type of restrictions above. There are no obvious examples for the employee suffering a disadvantage but this type of restriction attempts to cover any other eventuality. A not so unusual stance taken in the legislation to attempt to cover any possible scenario that may give rise to a challenge in particular cases. Just in case approach!

The restrictions are not limited to what may or may not be included in either the articles of association of the company or any shareholders agreement. The restrictions can be in the form of a contract, agreement, arrangement or condition. In other words, the arrangement may be an oral agreement in the form of a gentlemen's agreement and not in writing. It will still be a restriction subject to the regime. However, the restriction or restrictions must be present and affect the market value of the shares at the time the employee acquires the shares. Any restrictions added after acquisition will not fall within the regime.

It is very important to note though that some shares in a company may be inherently less valuable than other shares. For example, where the company has more than one class of shares, one class being ordinary shares that entitle the holders to any proceeds of sale and the second class being growth shares (discussed further later) that entitle the holder to any proceeds provided that the consideration for the sale of the shares exceeds a certain amount. The growth shares will be less valuable than the other ordinary shares in the company but, whilst they can be, will not necessarily be restricted.

The following restrictions do not fall within the regime:

- Any provision that allows the company to forfeit any of the shares held by an employee for non-payment of calls on unpaid or partly paid shares; and

- Compulsory transfer provisions in the company's articles of association often require employees to transfer their shares in the company on ceasing employment for misconduct.

*What are the tax consequences of restricted securities?*

Let us go back to Joanna and ABC Limited and consider the tax consequences by way of an example.

ABC Limited has just received valuation of the shares in the company. In order to be able to calculate the charge under the restricted securities regime, it is important to know both the AMV (or RMV) and the UMV. It is a lot more difficult to establish values few years down the line so it is highly recommended that, as a good practice, the two valuation are independently obtained whenever a transaction in shares is taking place.

Back to ABC Limited, it now has confirmation by independent valuers that the AMV of the shares is £5 per share and the UMV is £10 per share.

ABC Limited offers Joanna 100 ordinary shares at the AMV or £5 per share. Joanna accepts the offer and pays £500 to the company at the time that the UMV of the shares is £1,000. At this stage there are no tax implications as far as Joanna or the company is concerned. Had Joanna paid less than £5 per share, that would have been a transaction at undervalue and any benefit received by Joanna would have been subject to an immediate income tax on that benefit.

Just as a reminder, having considered the PAYE implications before, if at the time of the transaction, the shares are RCAs, the company will be required to operate the PAYE system in relation to any income tax charge. It will be required to deduct the correct amount of income tax including employee's NICs from Joanna's salary and pay it to HMRC together with the employer's NICs. If the shares are not RCAs then Joanna will be required to complete a self-assessment tax return and pay the income tax due on the benefit with no obligation on the company to operate the PAYE system and no NICs implications either for the company or for Joanna.

For the purpose of the example, we can assume that Joanna has just acquired ordinary shares that are subject to restrictions. The restricted securities regime, therefore, applies to the shares acquired by Joanna.

Joanna now has two options in relation to her acquisition of ordinary shares in ABC Limited and the restricted securities regime:

- One option is for Joanna to do nothing, just get on with her life and her participation in the company and hope for a good return on her investment when the company is eventually sold;
- The other option is for Joanna to immediately consider the inevitable tax implications that are lurking deep within the seemingly simple transaction of acquiring restricted shares in the company waiting for an opportunity to bite.

Let us consider the two options in more detail:

- Option one – do nothing

  Joanna does nothing. She has acquired ordinary shares in the company for their AMV of £5 per share. This is the true value of the shares at the time of acquisition given that they are subject to restrictions. The restrictions are very likely to be released in the future either because the company agrees to remove the restrictions or on a sale of the shares to an unconnected third-party buyer.

  Assuming that the shares in the company are sold five years later for £100 per share. The tax implications will be as follows:

  - looking back at the two valuations obtained by ABC Limited for the purpose of the sale of 100 shares to Joanna. The percentage difference between the AMV of £5 per share and the UMV of £10 per share is 50% or, in other words, Joanna's acquisition of shares in the company represents a 50% discount to the UMV of £10;

- when the shares are sold and the restrictions released, 50% of the UMV of the shares on the date of sale, which represent the untaxed portion of the shares acquired by Joanna, will be subject to income tax (the income tax will need to be operated by ABC Limited under the PAYE system, as, at that time, the shares are likely to be RCAs. Trading arrangements exist in relation to the shares in the company making them RCAs, i.e. the sale to an unconnected third-party) with the remainder of the gain being subject to CGT. Ouch!!!

- currently, the CGT rate of 20% is much lower than that of income tax which can be as high as 45%. Especially if Joanna can reduce any CGT liability further by the use of the ER the rate will be reduced to 10%. With the additional potential liability to NICs, it is very clear to see that Joanna may wish to avoid this option;

- in numbers 50% x £10,000 (being Joanna's sale proceeds) = £5,000 will be subject to income tax and NICs under the PAYE system;

- Joanna may have been under the impression that, on a sale of shares, any gain is subject to CGT. She may be very disappointed to find that a large amount of her gain is subject to income tax and NICs. On a sale of the shares, Joanna can, at least, afford to pay the tax due from the proceeds of sale. What if the occasion for charge is not a sale of the shares to an unconnected third-party but a variation or removal of the restrictions? Joanna will need to find the money to settle her tax liabilities. Being aware of the tax implications of doing nothing, Joanna has decided to consider the other option of doing something so that, perhaps, any tax implications are more bearable.

- Option two – do something

Joanna does not like the first option! There must be an alternative to simply doing nothing. Luckily, Joanna is told that, at the time she acquires the shares from ABC Limited and, in any event, within 14 days of acquisition of the shares by Joanna, both the employer, ABC Limited and Joanna can sign an election, electing to opt out of the restricted securities regime. Joanna thinks that anything that takes her out of the dreaded restricted securities regime must be a good option.

The election is known as a 'section 431(1) election'. When it is signed by the employer and employee, the employee agrees to pay income tax on that untaxed amount on acquisition or, in other words, on the amount representing the difference between the AMV and the UMV. In Joanna's case, if Joanna signs the election and pays income tax (which, at the time of acquisition may or may not be required to be operated under the PAYE system), any gain on disposal of her shares to an unconnected third-party will be subject to CGT only.

Given that Joanna has an option whether or not to sign the election she enquires further about the various implications of signing the section 431(1) election before she will make up her mind. She is warned that whilst the signing of the election means that she opts out of the restricted securities regime, in practical terms the following will need to be considered:

- income tax is payable on the difference between the amount that Joanna pays for the share i.e. £500 and the UMV of £1,000. Joanna will need to find the amount of income tax and possibly NICs to settle that liability;

- ○ if Joanna's is required by ABC Limited to transfer her shares back to the company or to someone else in accordance with the terms of the company's articles of association or shareholders' agreement, for the AMV of £500 or if, on a sale to an unconnected third-party buyer, the shares are not as valuable and are sold for, say, £5 per share, Joanna will not be able to get a refund of the income tax that she pays on acquisition.

This may not be an easy decision for Joanna to make. However, it may become easier for her, as in many cases, companies insist that employees sign the election. The tax implications on the lifting of the restrictions mean that the company itself may be faced with the obligation to operate the PAYE system in relation to the income tax liability. The company will need to deduct that money from the employee at a time when the employee may no longer be employed by the company. It will have a cost in respect of the employer's NICs that it may not, save for in specific circumstances, be able to pass to the employee.

If the company does not insist on the employee signing the election, the employee will need to consider the likelihood of the shares in the company becoming more valuable in the future, the prospect of a sale of the company or circumstances that may lead to the lifting of the restrictions. This may not be an easy decision but it will need to be made relatively quickly, as the election can be made within 14 days of the date the shares are acquired. The election is not required to be filed but can be kept with the company's statutory or other books as HMRC may wish to inspect it in the future.

Later, we will look at, and consider, the interaction between share schemes or share options and the restricted securities regime.

# CHAPTER FIVE
# EMPLOYEE BENEFIT TRUST (EBT)

An EBT is a form of discretionary trust which is established by companies in order to provide various benefits to their employees, former employees and their dependents.

Being a discretionary trust, the EBT and its trustees are independent from the company. The trustees of the company are appointed by the company. Anyone can be appointed but often the company will appoint professional or corporate trustees due to the administrative complexity of running the trust.

The company will normally recommend to the trustees of the EBT how the trustees should distribute any of the trust's income or assets or otherwise request that particular action is taken in respect of any of the employees of the company. However, being independent from the company, the trustees of the EBT are under a fiduciary duty to act in the best interests of the beneficiaries of the trust. Whilst the trustees, most probably, will act in accordance with the wishes of the company, they will do so by exercising their discretion after due and careful consideration of the interests of the beneficiaries as a whole.

With this in mind, a company may still wish to establish an EBT in order to create an internal market within the company and to facilitate the transfer of shares from employees or shareholders who leave the company in circumstances where they are required to sell their shares whether pursuant to the terms of the company's articles of association, shareholders agreement or otherwise.

The transfer of shares in private companies is, in most cases, subject to stringent restrictions which, in turn, may render any possibility of equity investment by employees in the company as an unattractive proposition. The setting up of an EBT will alleviate that concern and create a platform for a more seamless transfer of shares within the company which, can be viewed as an incentive for employees.

In the context of share schemes, company shares can be warehoused in the EBT in order to satisfy any share awards and to buy back shares from employees when they cease to be employees of the company or when they are required to sell under the terms of the relevant share scheme.

A UK resident EBT must be used when the company operates a Share Incentive Plan and, when the company operates a Joint Ownership Arrangement, the trustees of the EBT act as co-owners of shares in that arrangement.

The company will transfer shares into the EBT and fund it so that the trustees can carry out their obligations under the trust deed. The company will do so by transferring cash and other assets to the EBT by way of gift, loan or a combination of the two.

Taxation of EBTs

As any discretionary trust and given that the EBT is independent from the company that establishes the trust, the trustees of the EBT will be required to pay tax by reference to various transactions undertaken by the EBT. The liability of the trustees will depend on the residency of the trust. Companies often appoint trustees who are located offshore when the EBT accumulates capital assets that are subject to CGT. The basic tax implications of EBTs are as follows:

*Income tax liability?*

The trustees of a UK resident EBT are liable to pay, out of the trust fund, income tax on all of the EBT's income arising anywhere in the world whilst the income tax liability of non-UK resident EBTs is limited to UK source income only. For example, if a non-UK resident EBT holds shares in a UK company and receives dividends on those shares, the dividend income will be subject to income tax in the UK.

If accumulated income of the EBT is distributed to employees or other beneficiaries in circumstances where the relevant beneficiary pays income tax on the amount of the distribution, as, it forms part of the beneficiary's employment income, a UK resident EBT may be entitled to a relief from income tax on the amounts so distributed. A UK resident beneficiary may be entitled to claim a similar relief in respect of an income distribution by a non-UK resident EBT in similar circumstances.

*CGT liability?*

A UK resident EBT is subject to capital gains arising anywhere in the world so if the EBT disposes of shares or other capital asset located outside of the UK, the trustees of the EBT will be liable to pay CGT in respect of any gain arising from such disposals. On the other hand, non-UK resident EBTs are not liable to CGT in the UK.

If a capital asset of a UK resident EBT is transferred or otherwise distributed to employees or other beneficiaries in circumstances where the relevant beneficiary pays income tax on that distribution as it forms part of the beneficiary's employment income, the EBT may be entitled to a relief from CGT on the amounts so distributed.

*Inheritance tax liability?*

Inheritance tax is normally paid by reference to the value of the estate of an individual on the individual's death. However, inheritance tax may also be payable in respect of lifetime gifts which, may also include gifts made by the trustees of an EBT. The trustees of the EBT may be liable in circumstances where assets are gifted to beneficiaries or, for example, when shares are awarded to the company's employees at less than market value.

Most EBTs will be structured in a way that ensures that distributions by the trustees of the EBT are exempt from inheritance tax. The exemptions normally apply in circumstances where beneficiaries pay income tax on the distribution by the trustees. However, in certain circumstances inheritance tax may become an issue for the trustees of the EBT.

*Anti-avoidance?*

In the past, some EBTs have been set up by companies in order to provide benefits to employees or senior employees of the company whilst avoiding or attempting to avoid the payment of income tax and NICs on those benefits.

With effect from 6 April 2011, anti-avoidance legislation was introduced, referred to as the 'disguised remuneration' rules. The aim of the disguised remuneration rules is to prevent trustees and other third parties from providing any benefits to any employees or beneficiaries, which, otherwise, may be classified as employment income of those employees or beneficiaries, in circumstances whereby income tax and NICs liabilities are avoided.

The legislation imposes an immediate charge to income tax and NICs on a number of remuneration arrangements between third parties and employees. Such arrangements, which include benefits provided by EBTs, also include the earmarking or otherwise making available certain benefits to employees. Certain share scheme arrangements are excluded from charge but the disguised remuneration rules will need to be considered when benefits are provided to employees by any third party.

# CHAPTER SIX
# APPROVED SCHEMES VS. UNAPPROVED SCHEMES

We have already discussed the reasons for a company to wish to operate share or option schemes. In brief, equity ownership by employees incentivises and encourages employees to perform better for the company. In turn, the company benefits by becoming financially stronger, it is able to employ more people and provide better benefits to its employees. Overall, the employees, the company and the economy benefit from such investment by employees or senior employees.

There are two types of share or option schemes:

- Approved schemes or tax advantaged share schemes; and
- Unapproved schemes or non-tax advantaged share schemes.

*What is the difference between approved and unapproved schemes?*

- Approved schemes or tax advantaged share schemes -
    - these are schemes that are approved by HMRC and so provide favourable tax treatment to both employees and their employer. The tax benefits under approved schemes are normally limited to income tax and NICs and corporation tax deduction for the employer. Consequently, employment benefits received by employees in connection with share ownership in the company may be subject to a more favourable tax treatment allowing employees to acquire shares in the company where, otherwise, such acquisition may result in a financial strain on the employee;

- employees are liable to pay CGT on any gain that may arise on disposal of their shares in the company. There is no relief from the payment of CGT under the approved share schemes legislation other than in relation to one particular scheme, the Share Incentive Plan which, will be discussed later;

- obviously, to benefit from the favourable tax treatment, approved schemes can be used by companies and employees provided that both the company and its employees comply with certain conditions laid down by statute;

- as a result, approved schemes are less discretionary in nature but provide more certainty to both the company and its employees, as they use and follow specific statutory conditions, on which clearance can be received from HMRC in advance of entering into the relevant scheme.

- Unapproved schemes or non-tax advantaged share schemes –

    - as the name suggests, any share or option scheme that is not specifically approved by HMRC, is an unapproved scheme and, potentially subject to income tax and NICs on any benefit received by employees. Hence, non-tax advantaged share scheme;

    - being unapproved does not necessarily mean that the company or the employees are involved in any form of tax avoidance. It simply means that the relevant scheme does not need to be approved by HMRC, as it does not automatically benefit from any statutory tax reliefs (unless, of course, it can be structured in a tax efficient way);

- o given that they may not be as efficient as approved schemes, unapproved schemes are not subject to any statutory conditions. They are, therefore, much more flexible in terms of what can be agreed between the company and its employees. However, due to the fact that they cannot be pre-approved by HMRC, such schemes may be open to challenge by HMRC if they are perceived to have an avoidance motive as one of reasons for the setting up of the scheme by the company.

*Why do companies use unapproved schemes?*

Despite the fact that unapproved schemes may not afford employees with the most tax efficient way of ultimately acquiring shares in the company, there are few main reasons why companies may opt for unapproved schemes rather than the, perhaps, most logical, tax approved schemes:

- As has already been mentioned, approved schemes can be validly set up by companies if they comply with all relevant statutory conditions. We will look into the various conditions for each of the approved schemes later in the book. However, if either the company or the relevant employee is not able to comply with the conditions or any of them, that company may not be able to operate an approved scheme so may opt for an unapproved one;

- Unapproved schemes may be offered to those who may not be eligible to participate under approved schemes such as consultants and non-executive directors. However, the scheme will not be an employee's share scheme and may not get the benefit of the various company law and financial services exemptions. Whilst they may not be deemed to be employees of the company, so may not have the same tax issues that employees have, nonetheless, the company may wish to allow them to have an equity stake in the company. The company may wish to set up an unapproved scheme for such individuals rather than allow direct acquisition from the outset so that the company can stay in control of the timing of any new shareholders joining, which may be subject to various financial milestone or other individual performance conditions;

- Large public quoted companies commonly use unapproved schemes when they look to incentivise a select few senior executives, as any of the approved schemes are unlikely to be of interest to those senior executives. Such quoted companies still set up approved scheme but they normally set up approved schemes that apply to all employees of the company. Private companies are more likely to set up approved schemes for their senior executives. Only if they are insufficient or cause any of the conditions to be breached, they may use unapproved schemes as well. It is not as common for private companies to set up all employee approved schemes.

*What approved schemes are available?*

Only four approved schemes are available to companies. They are:

- Enterprise Management Incentive (EMI);
- Company Share Option Plan (CSOP);
- Save As You earn (SAYE); and
- Share Incentive Plan (SIP).

The first two schemes, the EMI and CSOP schemes allow for greater flexibility than the other two schemes, The SAYE and SIP schemes. They do not have to be offered to all of the employees of the company and can even be set up in order to incentivise one employee but care must be taken to ensure that it falls within the definition of employees' option scheme. In terms of financial reward, employees can expect to receive a much higher reward with the first two schemes, as the other schemes provide a relatively low value reward.

The first two schemes are therefore more popular with private companies whilst the latter two schemes are mainly used by large public quoted companies that may wish to offer such schemes to all of their employees as one of the many benefits they may provide.

*What unapproved schemes are available?*

As there are no statutory tax reliefs for any of the unapproved schemes, unapproved schemes provide greater flexibility for both the company and its employees. There is no need to be concerned with the type of shares, any financial limits, the size of the company or even the identity of the employee (in terms of employment status). Therefore, other than any legal or regulatory requirements, there are no restrictions or any conditions placed on any of the unapproved schemes.

The starting point is that they are fully taxable unless they can be structured in a tax efficient way. There are, therefore, many different types of unapproved schemes, each with its own tax consequences. Some are structured in a tax efficient way so that employees can afford to acquire shares in the company. Other unapproved schemes are subject to tax when they are exercised so they are structured in a way that allows exercise on an exit or, in other words, on a sale of the company so that employees can get value from which to pay the exercise price and any tax due on exercise.

It is important to remember that, in relation to an option scheme, being an option, the option holder is under no obligation to exercise the option at any time. When the option holder is able to exercise the option, at that time, the option holder will need to consider the amount payable on exercise together with any tax liability and, of course, the actual market value of the shares on the date of exercise. If the shares are being sold on exercise, the disposal proceeds on exercise. If, having considered the various values, an exercise makes financial sense, then the option may be exercised. If not, the option holder may wish to do nothing and simply let the option lapse so that it becomes incapable of being exercised.

Some of the most popular unapproved schemes include:

- Bonus Scheme/Phantom Option Scheme;
- Share Option Scheme;
- Joint Ownership Arrangement;
- Growth Shares;
- Nil Paid Shares; and
- Long Term Incentive Plan (LTIP).

# CHAPTER SEVEN
# EMPLOYEES' SHARE SCHEMES

Companies often offer their employees share options or other share schemes in order to incentivise them by enabling them to participate in the ownership of the company so that they are encouraged to help build the business of the company, as such ownership may result in them being financially rewarded for their efforts.

Tax advantaged schemes or approved schemes have been designed by legislation to encourage companies to allow their employees to participate in the ownership of the company. Such participation helps motivate employees to do more for the business of the company, help the company grow and in return reward the employees for their efforts. Overall, growing and more successful companies employ more people and ultimately benefit the economy as a whole.

For this reason, the government is encouraging the participation of employees by easing some of the compliance and administrative burdens that companies may encounter when share or options schemes interact with company law and/or financial services regulations.

Company law provisions relating to pre-emption and share buyback restrictions and directors' authority to allot shares in the company are relaxed when the scheme is an employees' share scheme. Company law also includes, amongst other things, provisions that allow a public company to give financial assistance, in certain circumstances, to its employees for the acquisition of shares by the employees. Such provisions are normally required to be complied with by the company before financial assistance can be validly and legally given. However, some of the provisions are relaxed if financial assistance is given in connection with an employees' share scheme.

Likewise, some of the financial services regulations, in connections with the promotion of, or dealing with, shares in the company, will not apply to a company that issues shares to its employees under an employees' share scheme.

In order to get the benefit of various company law and financial services regulations exemptions in connection with the relevant scheme, which, make the setting up and implementation of the scheme much easier in terms of compliance and administrative burden, the option or share scheme will need to be structured in such a way as to enable it to fall within the statutory definition of 'employees' share scheme'.

'Employees' share scheme' is defined as follows:

"an employees' share scheme is a scheme for encouraging or facilitating the holding of shares in or debentures of a company by or for the benefit of:

- the bona fide employees or former employees of:
    - the company,
    - any subsidiary of the company, or
    - the company's holding company or any subsidiary of the company's holding company, or
- the spouses, civil partners, surviving spouses, surviving civil partners, or minor children or step-children of such employees or former employees."

This means that a scheme operated by a company for the benefit of its employees will most probably fall within the definition of employees' share scheme. However, a scheme that allows consultants or non-executive directors, who are not employees, former employees or dependents of such employees, to participate in the company's option or share scheme may jeopardise the benefit of any of the exemptions that are normally available to companies that operate schemes that fall within the definition.

Companies can still consider issuing shares to non-employees under the umbrella of a share scheme but must then make sure that they comply with all relevant company law and financial services regulations that apply to the issue of shares in the company, as the exemptions afforded for an employees' share scheme may not be available to the company. If shares are issued to both employees and non-employees, companies should consider setting up two separate schemes in order to ensure that the scheme as a whole does not infringe the definition referred to above.

Whilst a scheme can be operated by a company for one employee, it is important for the company to make sure that, in order to fall within the definition, the scheme allows participation of other employees in the future. Being a scheme, it can be understood that it must be available for more than one employee, otherwise it may not be regarded as a scheme but, simply, the issue of shares outside of a scheme with the various exemptions not being available.

# CHAPTER EIGHT
# KEY TERMS USED IN SHARE SCHEMES

The following terms are used in respect of all schemes, whether approved or unapproved:

- **Grant**

  An award to employees of an option to acquire shares in the company;

- **Exercise**

  An option realised and option holder becomes a shareholder in the company;

- **Exit only**

  Options that are only capable of being exercised on a sale of the shares or business of the company;

- **Vest**

  Options are capable of being exercised. Options may only be capable of being exercised after a period of time or subject to conditions, during which time the options are unvested, as they are incapable of being exercised;

- **Lapse**

  Option comes to an end and can no longer be exercised;

- **Optionholder**

  An eligible employee who is granted options under the scheme;

- **Good Leaver**
    - o death;
    - o leaving employment due to:
        - ▪ injury;
        - ▪ disability;
        - ▪ redundancy;
        - ▪ retirement;
        - ▪ a TUPE transfer;
        - ▪ the employer company ceasing to be an associated company.

- **Constituent Company**

  A group company, the employees of which may be nominated to participate in a CSOP scheme by the scheme organiser;

- **Participant**

  A qualifying employee who is granted options under the scheme;

- **Scheme Organiser**

  The company that establishes a scheme. In a group, options may be granted in respect of shares in another company within the group and not necessarily in the scheme organiser.

# CHAPTER NINE
# APPROVED SCHEMES

## Enterprise Management Incentive (EMI)

The EMI scheme is possibly the most popular scheme for small to medium sized private trading companies. It is specifically aimed at high risk private companies and in return for employees or senior employees accepting awards under the EMI scheme, they can expect to receive generous tax benefits on exercise. The scheme's effectiveness in achieving the desired results for both companies and their employees has been confirmed by HMRC.

The EMI Scheme is also very popular because of its flexibility. Provided that a company can validly set up an EMI scheme in terms of that company complying with certain statutory requirements in respect of the company, the relevant employees and the shares under the scheme and subject to satisfaction by the company of certain requirements relating to the options to be awarded under the scheme, the scheme can be drafted to suit any arrangement between the company and any of its employees.

Being an option, the employee has a choice whether to exercise the option or not. Any financial commitment on the part of the employee will normally arise on the exercise of the option by the employee paying the exercise price. Until then the option is risk-free to the employee.

*Does the company qualify for EMI?*

The starting point for a company that considers the setting up of an EMI scheme, is to consider the statutory requirements that apply to the company or, in other words, if the company can demonstrate that it satisfies the following requirements, it will be able to set up an EMI scheme for the benefit of its employees.

The company requirements:

- The company must be **independent** –

This condition, whilst seemingly simple and straightforward, may not be so when the meaning of independence is further considered. The statutory provision states that for the company to be independent, two conditions must be satisfied in relation to that company:

  - the first condition is that the company must not be a 51% subsidiary of another company or, in circumstances where the company is not a 51% subsidiary of another company, it must not be under the control of another company and another person who is connected with that other company;

  - the second condition is that no arrangements are in existence for the company to become either a 51% of another company or under the control of that other company.

The first part of the first condition is breached in relatively straight forward circumstances where more than 50% of the company's ordinary share capital is owned by another corporate. There are some complicated group structures in existence but not too difficult to trace the correct ownership in order to determine the company's independence. When this part of the condition is considered, one needs to consider the shareholding in the company.

However, the more difficult one to ascertain relates to the second part of the first condition. Under the second part of the first condition, the company may not be owned by any corporate in circumstances where the first part of the first condition is breached but may be under the control of another company and any other person connected with that other company. When this part of the condition is considered, one needs to consider other forms of control that may influence the running or working of the company.

Essentially, a person is said to control a company if that person and anyone connected with that person control the company in circumstances where the company's affairs are conducted in accordance with the wishes of that person whether by reason of that person's shareholding in the company or because the articles of association of the company, any other document or otherwise confer on that person any such right.

The company that is considering its independence may breach that part of the first condition if it is under the control of an associated company or even of a company that has a minority shareholding in the company. A simple example is where no decision can be taken by any director of the company without it being sanctioned by a bank due to the existence of a loan by that bank to the company. In order to ensure that the company is independent, one will need to ensure that the company is not controlled by any such person.

In regard to the second condition, the company will not be independent if any arrangements exit, at the time that the independence requirement is considered for EMI purposes, for the company to become a subsidiary of another company or to be under the control of another company. If no such arrangements exist then the company may be independent but any future loss of independence may impact on an EMI scheme within the company. This will be considered further later on in this chapter.

An EMI scheme can only be set up by an independent company. This means that in a group structure, it is the parent company that can set up an EMI scheme and grant options either to its own employees or to employees of any of its subsidiaries so that they acquire shares in the parent company.

This requirement may be very inconvenient for some international groups. For example, an organisation may wish to benefit a senior employee who works for a UK subsidiary, by awarding him or her EMI options in the UK subsidiary. The intention is to benefit that senior employee in respect of the UK business and not the overall business of the group. Whilst inconvenient, the EMI option must only be set up in the parent but with some clever drafting to the rights attaching to the class of shares, the subject of the EMI options, so that they only benefit the holder from any value arising from the UK subsidiary.

- The company must be a **trading** company –

The company must be a trading company and in a group structure at least one company within the group must be carrying on a qualifying trade. Again, this requirement seems very simple to follow. Most companies and their advisers know the difference between trading and investment companies so, as long as the company is not an investment company, this requirement can be ticked as satisfied by the trading company. Well not so quickly as it is not as simple as it seems!

When one is looking at the trading requirement, two issues will need to be carefully considered:

- Firstly, the company must carry on a qualifying trade. A qualifying trade is:
    - a trade undertaken on a commercial basis with a view to making profits; and
    - very importantly, a trade that does not, to a substantial extent, include any activities that are not qualifying trading activities.

HMRC interprets 'substantial' as meaning 20% or more. This means that a company that carries on a qualifying trade but 20% or more of its overall activities are carried out other than for the purpose of the qualifying trade or trades, will not be a trading company or the holding company of a trading group for EMI purposes.

HMRC will consider each case on its own merits. Any non-qualifying activities will be considered by reference to the company's turnover, its capital or any other appropriate measure depending on the type of company, the industry to which it belongs and the way that company conducts its business.

For example, a company that generates a substantial amount of cash may not distribute all or most of it to its shareholders. The company's cash reserves may amount to more than 20% of the company's, say, turnover. If the company can demonstrate, by recording it in board minutes, that it intends to use the money for future expansion or generally for the purpose of the trade, then a solid investment of that money in the short term may not impact on the company's trading status. On the other hand, if the company uses the money to invest in the acquisition of an office block which it lets on a commercial basis or if a director of the company spends a lot of his or her time looking into high risk or other investments then such activities may jeopardise the company's trading status.

- Secondly, given the impossibility of defining the type of trades that may qualify for EMI purposes, it is a lot easier to define a qualifying trade by reference to the excluded ones. Therefore, the company's activities must not be included within any one or more of the following excluded activities, which by statute, have been specifically excluded from operating EMI schemes. The excluded activities are:

    - dealing in land, commodities or futures, shares, securities or other financial instruments;

    - dealing in goods, otherwise than in the course of an ordinary trade of wholesale or retail distribution;

    - banking, insurance, money-lending, debt-factoring, hire purchase financing or other financial activities;

- leasing including letting ships on charter, or other assets on hire;
- receiving royalties or other licence fees;
- providing legal or accountancy services;
- property development;
- farming or market gardening;
- holding, managing or occupying woodlands, any other forestry activities or timber production;
- shipbuilding;
- producing coal;
- producing steel;
- operating or managing hotels or comparable establishments, such as a guesthouse or hostel, or managing property used as a hotel or comparable establishment;
- operating or managing nursing homes or residential care homes, or managing property used as a nursing home or residential care home;
- providing services or facilities for a business carried on by another person if the business consists to a substantial extent of excluded activities and a controlling interest in the business is held by a person who also has a controlling interest in the business carried on by the company providing the services or facilities.

- The company must only have **qualifying subsidiaries** –

In a group structure, for a subsidiary to be a qualifying subsidiary, it must be more than 50% beneficially owned by the parent. The holding by the parent can be direct holding or indirect via other subsidiaries. It must be controlled by the parent or by any of its qualifying subsidiaries but by no other person and, as usual, there must be no arrangements in place under which any of the shareholding or control requirements will cease to be applied to the group.

Where the subsidiary's main business is the holding or managing land, the parent is required to have a direct holding of at least 90% of the ordinary share capital in that subsidiary. That holding must be translated to both voting powers in the subsidiary and a beneficial entitlement by the parent company to any profits that may be available for distribution to shareholders and assets that may be available on a winding up of the subsidiary.

A group structure that includes a joint venture company as the only or one of the subsidiaries of the group, may be a stumbling block on the parent company's ability to set up an EMI scheme for the benefit of its employees. It may be possible, in some cases, to agree to change the shareholding in the joint venture company so that it is a qualifying subsidiary for the purpose of the EMI legislation.

The company may, for commercial reasons and not for tax avoidance reasons, alter any of its shareholding or do anything so that the subsidiaries are all qualifying subsidiaries at or before the date the EMI scheme is set up. The EMI scheme will not be invalidated if any of the subsidiaries of the company ceases to be a qualifying subsidiary after the setting up of the scheme.

- The company's **gross assets** –

The company's gross assets must not exceed £30 million. Within a group structure, the gross assets value is looked at by reference to the whole group. Given that the EMI scheme encourages employees to invest in the company so that the company grows, employs more people and ultimately more tax is payable for the benefit of the economy as a whole, the gross assets value must be taken on the date of grant of the EMI options. If the company's gross assets value is exceeded at any point after the grant of options under the EMI scheme, the validity of the scheme will not be affected.

The EMI scheme is aimed at small and medium sized companies so most enterprises may be well within that limit. In most cases companies will not be required to do anything other than confirm that they are within the limit. However, some companies may be uncertain as to whether their gross value falls just below or over the gross assets value. A company that faces such an uncertainty may need to prepare a balance sheet as at the date the EMI option is granted so that the company's confirmation of its compliance with this requirement is correct.

- The company's **employees** –

The company must have fewer than 250 full-time equivalent employees. The same applies within a group structure so a head count of all employees of the parent and its qualifying subsidiaries may need to be undertaken by reference to the full-time equivalent employees.

*What does full-time equivalent mean?*

HMRC counts an employee to be a full-time employee if that employee works for 35 hours or more per week. Two part-time employees who together work for 35 hours per week will be counted as one full-time employee and so on.

As with the gross assets value requirement above, as the overall intention is for companies to grow, the limit on the number of employees is only relevant at the date of grant of EMI options. Once the scheme is set up any increase to the number of employees will not affect the validity of the scheme and any of the EMI tax benefits.

Again, as with the gross assets value requirement above, in most cases a company will be able to confirm its compliance with this requirement as most will probably have fewer than 250 full-time equivalent employees. However, when uncertain, the company will need to undertake a review of the number of its full-time employees and any full-time equivalent employees. Directors are included and counted as employees but employees on maternity, paternity or shared parental leave or students on vocational training are excluded and are not counted as employees towards the number of 250 employees limit.

- The company's **UK connection** –

The company must have a permanent establishment in the UK. In the case of a UK resident company, this will not be an issue. However, where the parent company of a group is not a UK resident company, at least one of its qualifying subsidiaries must have a permanent establishment in the UK.

*What can the company do in case of uncertainty?*

Given the complexity of some of the company requirements, more particularly but not limited to the independence and trading status of the company, it is possible for the company to seek advance clearance from HMRC that the company complies with the requirements above so that the company may have certainty as to the validity of the EMI scheme.

However, companies may not always want to take advantage of the advance clearance and may wish to rely on their own or their advisers' assessment of the requirements. In any event, it is important to consider the ability to seek advance clearance in cases of real uncertainty and complexity.

The employee requirements:

EMI options can only be awarded to eligible employees of the company or, where the company is the parent company of a group, of that parent company or a qualifying subsidiary of the parent company.

*Who is an eligible employee?*

- **Working time** requirement –

To be an eligible employee, the employee is required to work for the relevant company for at least:

- 25 hours per week; or
- If the employee works for less than 25 hours per week, to be eligible, he or she must work for the relevant company for at least 75% of his or her overall working time.
    - the employees' working time includes any time spent by that employees as an employee or self-employed person;
    - therefore, if the employee works only for the relevant company for, say, 10 hours per week, the employee will be an eligible employee for EMI purposes as this time represents 100% of his working time. However, if, on the other hand, the employee works for the relevant company for 10 hours per week and for another company for 20 hours per week, his or her working time for the relevant company will be less than 75% of his or her overall working time so will not be an eligible employee.
- No **material interest** requirement –

To be an eligible employee, the employee must not have a material interest in the company or, where the company is the parent company of a group, of that parent company or any subsidiary of the parent company.

An employee has a material interest in the relevant company if the employee has a beneficial ownership of, or an entitlement to acquire, more than 30% of the ordinary share capital, or, where the relevant company is a close company, of the assets of the relevant company or has the ability to control more than 30% either directly or indirectly by any other means.

The employee is treated as having a material interest in the relevant company if, together with any one or more of the employee's associates, the employee has a material interest in the relevant company or if any one or more of the employee's associates have a material interest in the relevant company.

Associates include any relatives of the employee so, for example, if the relevant company is 100% owned by the employee's father. The father wants to grant EMI options to his son but as the father is an associate of the employee, the employee is treated as having a material interest in the company so will not be able to be granted EMI options.

The EMI options requirements:

- **Purpose** requirement –

For the EMI option to be valid, the purpose of the EMI options must be to grant EMI options to employees of the company for commercial reasons in order to recruit or retain employees in the relevant company. The options must not be granted as part of a scheme or arrangement the main purpose or one of the main purposes of which is the avoidance of tax.

- **Individual limit** requirement –

The relevant company may grant to any one employee options to acquire not more than £250,000 worth of shares. The value is calculated by reference to the market value of the shares (ignoring any restrictions on those shares) at the date of grant. Any options granted in excess of the £250,000 limit will not be valid EMI options and, on exercise, the employee will not receive any tax benefit on any shares that exceed that limit.

It is very important to note that, once granted, the employee cannot be granted any more valid EMI options within the three years period from the date of the first grant. It makes no difference whether the employee was first granted options with a value below the £250,000 limit or whether any of the options have been exercised or lapsed within that period.

- **Company limit** requirement –

The relevant company can issue not more than £3 million worth of shares, the subject of any unexercised EMI options. The value is calculated by reference to the market value of the shares (ignoring any restrictions on those shares) at the date of grant. Any options granted in excess of the £3 million limit will not be valid EMI options and, on exercise, the employee will not receive any tax benefit on any shares that exceed that limit.

- **Options** requirement –

The EMI options must entitle the employee to acquire ordinary shares in the capital of the relevant company. The shares must be fully paid up and not redeemable. On exercise of the options, the employee can be allotted new shares in the relevant company. Alternatively, the options cam be satisfied by a transfer of shares by any shareholder (including an Employee Benefit Trust).

In order to ensure that the EMI scheme remains an incentive for employees, the options must be capable of being exercised within the period of 10 years from the date of grant. If the options are exercised after the period of 10 years, the employee will lose any tax benefits.

The EMI option must be in writing either by way of a standalone contract between the relevant company and the employee or as plan rules out of which the company can issue separate contract to employees at different times.

Either way, any such written agreement must state:

- The date of grant;
- That it is an EMI option pursuant to the relevant statutory provisions;
- The number of shares that may be acquired under the scheme;
- The exercise price;
- When the option can be exercised and how;
- If the exercise is subject to performance conditions, the conditions;
- If the shares are restricted securities, the restrictions must be clearly set out in the agreement;
- That the options must not be transferred to any other person.

*What is next?*

Now that we have established the various requirements relating to the company, the employee and the options, and on the basis that the company is satisfied that it is able to set up an EMI scheme, the company can start the process of setting up the EMI scheme.

Share valuation

Shares in the company need to be valued for the purpose of the EMI scheme. Valuation of the shares is not a statutory requirement but is highly recommended. Valuation of the shares helps determine the exercise price and is necessary to determine the income tax liability of the employee if the EMI options or part of them lose their EMI status and end up being subject to income tax.

HMRC will agree a valuation based on the AMV or RMV and the UMV of the shares. The valuation is valid for 90 days during which time EMI options will need to be granted to employees. If EMI options are not granted within the 90 days period, the company may contact HMRC and either confirm that nothing has changed in the company so that the original valuation may be reconfirmed by HMRC for an additional period of 90 days or agree a new valuation on the basis that the value of the shares in the company has changed during this time whether up or down.

The company may use the AMV as the exercise price or any amount above that amount. If EMI options are granted at an exercise price of less than the AMV, the amount below the AMV will be subject to an immediate charge to income tax on the date of exercise of the options. Unlike with other approved options, it is important to note that whilst the individual limit of £250,000 is calculated by reference to the UMV, the exercise price may be calculated by reference to the AMV or RMV for the favourable taxable benefits to be obtained in full.

Granting EMI options

Once valuation of the shares in the company has been agreed with HMRC, the company is ready to complete the drafting of the EMI scheme and grant EMI options to its eligible employees.

Working time declaration

The employee must sign a working time declaration confirming compliance with the working time requirement. A copy of the declaration must be retained by the company and provided to the employee within seven days. The employee's failure to make the working time declaration may lose the tax benefits associated with the EMI scheme. For convenience, the declaration may be included within the EMI option agreement.

Notifications

Following the grant of EMI options to eligible employees, the company must notify HMRC within 92 days. The notification must be done online through the ERS online filing system. Failure to notify within the 92 days period will result in the scheme becoming invalid and no longer subject to any tax benefits.

The notification includes a declaration by the company that:

- The relevant EMI statutory provisions have been satisfied;

- The option holder has signed the working time declaration, a copy of which is held by the company.

The company is also required to complete online annual returns. All annual returns must be submitted by 6 July after the end of the relevant tax year. The company must notify any changes to the scheme including exercise of options, release or lapse of options, any exchange of options or any other adjustment to any of the EMI options. The company must complete the annual return even if there have been no changes that require notification.

Tax Implications

*For the Company –*

Provided that all relevant requirements are complied with, the company will be entitled to a corporation tax deduction in connection with the EMI scheme. The company can deduct an amount equal to the benefit obtained by the employee when the options are exercised. This is the most valuable deduction the company can get in connection with the scheme. However, if the company wishes to get a deduction for the amounts spent on setting up the scheme and the operation of the scheme throughout its life, the company may need to rely on either specific statutory provisions or under general principles.

The setting up of the scheme is considered to be capital in nature and therefore not deductible. However, the operation of the scheme may be deductible under general principles.

In a group structure, the employee may exercise options to acquire shares in the parent company whilst being employed by one of the parent's subsidiaries. The corporation tax deduction can only be claimed by the employer company and not by the company in which the employee acquires shares.

The corporation tax deduction can only be claimed in the accounting period in which shares are allotted or transferred to the employee, which, normally, occurs in the accounting period when the exercise of the options takes place.

*For the employee –*

Provided that all relevant conditions, requirements and notifications have been complied with by both the company and the option holder, the following expected tax implications will arise on exercise of the EMI options.

*On the date of grant?*

There are no tax implications when options are granted to eligible employees.

*On exercise?*

*Income tax liability?*

There is no income tax liability when EMI options are exercised at the AMV or RMV (or any higher amount) of the shares as at the date of grant. If EMI options are granted at an exercise price of less than the

AMV, the amount below the AMV will be subject to an immediate charge to income tax on the date of exercise of the options. This is because that amount represents an acquisition at an undervalue or at a discount to the AMV, which benefit is not included within the EMI legislation.

*NICs liability?*

Given that exercise of the shares does not give rise to a liability to income tax, there's also no liability to NICs. This is because NICs liability usually follows that of income tax but only in circumstances where the shares are readily convertible assets.

If an income tax liability arises in connection with the exercise of the shares in circumstances where the employer company is required to operate the PAYE system and deduct the amount of income tax from the employee together with primary Class 1 NICs. The employer will need to pay to HMRC the amount deducted together with the secondary Class 1 NICs. However, the employer may recover its liability in respect of the secondary Class 1 NICs from the employee. It can do so either by way of recovery from the employee or by transferring it to the employee.

*Are the shares restricted securities?*

The shares acquired following exercise of the EMI options are very likely to be restricted securities. Indeed, the shares may have been acquired at an exercise price that represents the AMV or RMV. Does this then mean that, in order to avoid the restricted securities regime, the employee needs to consider signing the section 431(1) election?

There is an obvious interaction between the EMI legislation providing an income tax relief on exercise and the restricted securities regime. The fact that restricted securities can be acquired under the EMI scheme in circumstances where no income tax liability arises on exercise does not mean that the restricted securities regime can simply be ignored.

All good, as this issue has not been left untouched. Normally, the employee acquiring restricted securities will need to consider the implications of the restricted securities regime. As a reminder, the employee will have two options:

- Sign the section 431(1) election within 14 days of acquisition so that any benefit received by the employee that represents the difference between the AMV and the UMV is charged to income tax and is payable on acquisition of the restricted securities. In which case any gain on disposal is subject to CGT only; or

- Not sign the election but then any disposal proceeds are multiplied by a percentage that represents the difference between the AMV and the UMV on acquisition and that amount is subject to income tax and possibly NICs on disposal of the shares.

When restricted shares are acquired following exercise of EMI options, the employee does not need to consider the two options above, as the legislation provides a deeming provision in connection with the section 431(1) election. So effectively, the employee is deemed to have signed the election (more like, a statutory election) and, as a consequence, any gain on disposal of the restricted shares will only be subject to CGT.

Sounds great, a weight off the employee's shoulder. One less thing to worry about. Hmm, not quite. The legislation also provides that the deeming provision falls away if income tax is payable on exercise of the options. Income tax may be payable on exercise if the EMI options are exercised at less than the AMV or if there is a disqualifying event in relation to the options (more on this very shortly).

The obvious solution is for the employee to sign the election in any event. Even if the company and the employee are not aware of any disqualifying events, on a future inspection, it may be resolved that income tax should have been paid on exercise. By then, it will be too late for the employee to sign the section 431(1) election. Employers often insist that employees sign the section 431(1) election on exercise so whilst the deeming provision is something that is nice to have, if the employee fails to sign the election, in many cases both companies and employees do not rely on that deeming provision.

*On disposal of the shares?*

When the shares are ultimately sold or otherwise disposed of by the employee, either immediately following exercise of the options or after a period of ownership, CGT may be payable by the employee on any gain. CGT is due if the sale proceeds exceed the price that the employee paid on exercise of the options.

Any amount on which income tax is paid by the employee together with any liability of the employer to Class 1 NICs that is transferred to the employee is added to the base cost of the shares. For example, an exercise price of less than the AMV as of the date of grant will result in an income tax charge on the difference between the price paid on exercise and the AMV. Whilst the employee has paid an amount on exercise which is less than the AMV, the base cost for CGT purposes will be the AMV.

*Will the employee qualify for ER?*

The employee may qualify for ER in respect of the gain provided that the employee can demonstrate that he or she was an employee of the relevant company and that he or she owned the shares (including the period in which options were held) for at least two years ending with the date of disposal of the shares.

The requirement for the holding of at least 5% of the share capital is no longer relevant to employees acquiring shares in the company under the EMI scheme. Therefore, most holders of shares following the exercise of their EMI options may be entitled to claim ER on disposal of their shares in the company.

## Disqualifying events

### *What is a disqualifying event?*

Previously, we looked at the requirements for a valid EMI scheme. Some of the requirements must be strictly observed and continue to be met throughout the life of the scheme. This is not so simple, as directors of the company may need to be aware of the requirements and any events or transactions that may cause a potential breach or non-compliance with the requirements. The disqualifying events are therefore requirements for a valid EMI scheme that are not complied with until the EMI scheme has come to an end. The disqualifying events are:

- Loss of independence. Save in circumstances where the buyer or new parent company allows the employees to exchange their EMI options for replacement options in the new parent company;

- Loss of trading status. This is probably the most breached requirement, given the potential complexity of understanding or even realising that the company may have investments that may exceed the 20% threshold. Directors may not be aware that such investments may have an impact on the trading status of the company;

- Working time requirements. The employee may choose to increase his or her self-employment or may take another employment with another unconnected employer and reduce his or her working time for the company to less than 75% of his or her overall working time;

- Cessation of employment. If the employee is no longer employed by any of the group companies, a disqualifying event will be triggered. There is a different treatment for an employee who dies in service, as the legislation allows the employee's personal representatives to exercise the options within the period of one year of the employee's death;

- Variation to the terms of the EMI option. Some variations may not impact on the scheme so may not be considered disqualifying events. However, some variations may be so fundamental that they may impact on the rights and obligations of the parties to such an extent that the changes may be treated as the cancellation of the scheme and the grant of a new option;

- Alteration of the share capital in circumstances where such change impacts on the value of the shares resulting in the some of the requirements for a valid EMI scheme not being met.

*Not a disqualifying event?*

The following requirements for a valid EMI scheme are only relevant at the time options are granted to employees. The relevant company is not required to comply with any of them after the date of grant. This is because companies are expected to grow and such growth cannot be allowed to impact on the validity of the scheme. However, if the company considers the grant of any additional EMI options, the following requirements will need to be satisfied at the time the second grant of options takes place. The following are therefore not disqualifying events:

- Gross assets exceeding £30M;

- A subsidiary ceasing to be a qualifying subsidiary;

- Option holder acquiring a material interest;

- Company employing more than 250 employees.

*What is the effect of a disqualifying event?*

Whilst:

- A failure to notify HMRC within 92 days of the date of grant results in the scheme losing its qualifying status so, effectively, no favourable tax treatment is due on exercise;

- An exercise after 10 years of the date of grant of EMI options loses any favourable tax treatment,

a disqualifying event will result in a partial loss of the income tax benefits under the scheme.

As soon as a disqualifying event occurs, the employee can exercise his or her options within 90 days in order to retain the favourable tax treatment under the EMI scheme. Any exercise after the 90 days period will result in any benefit arising (the rise in value of the shares) in the period between the date on which the disqualifying event occurs and actual exercise of the options to be subject to income tax and NICs.

Also, ER will be lost if the option is exercised after the 90 days period or if the exercise takes place within the 90 days period but within the first two years of the date of grant, as the employee will not have the requisite two years period.

## Company Share Option Plan (CSOP)

A CSOP scheme is a discretionary option scheme under which companies may grant options to any number of employees over ordinary shares in the company. As with any other option scheme, the option is risk free to the employees. There is no initial financial commitment on the part of the employee and no obligation to exercise the option in the future. An exercise price will be payable by the employee when the option is exercised.

A company operating a CSOP scheme does not have to comply with all of the same requirements as that operating an EMI scheme. For example, the company does not have to be a trading company or have any restrictions by reference to its size, the size of its workforce or ownership of its subsidiaries. For this reason, the CSOP scheme is very useful where the company is not able to operate an EMI scheme.

*What is the purpose of the CSOP?*

It is a statutory requirement for a CSOP scheme to provide benefits to directors and employees in the form of a share option. There must be no other benefit under the scheme and no cash equivalent is allowed. Any cash payment will be treated as a bonus and subject to income tax and NICs in the usual way.

*Which company can set up a CSOP?*

To qualify, a company must be either listed on a recognised stock exchange or be independent. However, the company is still independent if it is controlled by a corporate trustee of an employee ownership trust.

*Who can participate in a CSOP?*

- **Employment** requirement –

Any employee of the company or of the group may participate in a CSOP scheme. Unlike under the EMI scheme, the employee can be either full-time or part-time employee. Directors may also participate in the scheme but they have to be full-time directors. HMRC has confirmed that full-time directors must work for the company or the group for at least 25 hours per week.

Consultants, non-executive directors and those using service companies are excluded and cannot participate in a CSOP scheme.

- No **material interest** requirement –

An employee is not able to participate in a CSOP scheme on any date if that employee has, or had at any time within the period of 12 months ending on that date, a material interest in a close company which is one of the following:

- The company in which shares are acquired for the purpose of the CSOP scheme;
- A company that controls the company in which CSOP shares are acquired or a member of a consortium that owns a company that controls the company in which CSOP shares are acquired.

An employee has a material interest in the relevant company if the employee has a beneficial ownership of, or an entitlement to acquire, more than 30% (25% prior to 17 of July 2013) of the ordinary share capital of the relevant company or has the ability to control more than 30% either directly or indirectly by any other means.

The employee is treated as having a material interest in the relevant company if, together with any one or more of the employee's associates, the employee has a material interest in the relevant company or if any one or more of the employee's associates have a material interest in the relevant company.

Associates include any relatives of the employee so, for example, if the employee's brother owns 40% of the ordinary share capital of the relevant company, the employee will not be able to participate in the CSOP scheme as the brother is an associate of the employee. The employee is, therefore, treated as having a material interest in the company so will not be able to be granted CSOP options.

For EMI purposes, the material interest requirement is required to be met only on the date of grant. However, for CSOP purposes, the material interest requirement must be met throughout the life of the CSOP scheme. Therefore, the employee will not be able to exercise the CSOP options if on the exercise date the employee has, or, in the preceding 12 months period, has had a material interest.

*What is the individual limit?*

The maximum value of the shares, as at the date of grant, is £30,000 for any one employee. The value is calculated by reference to the market value of the shares (ignoring any restrictions on those shares) at the date of grant. Any shares that, at the date of grant, exceed that amount will be treated as unapproved and not subject to the tax benefits afforded under the CSOP scheme. Unlike the EMI scheme, if the value of the CSOP options exceed the individual limit of £30,000, the options will not be CSOP options but unapproved options in relation to the whole amount.

It is therefore important to ensure that the individual limit is not exceeded. In determining whether or not the individual limit is exceeded, the following scenario we'll need to be considered, where relevant. If a participant is granted CSOP options at a market value of, say, £4 and a year later that participant is granted a second CSOP options at the then market value of £3, both values will need to be aggregated by reference to the relevant market value at the time the

CSOP options are granted. The market value of the first grant is not reduced, for the purpose of the calculation, only because the market value of the shares has gone down.

Options which have been exercised by the participant, surrendered or lapsed do not count towards the £30,000 individual limit. Otherwise, all unexercised CSOP options will need to be aggregated.

Other requirements:

- **Shares** requirement –

The participant must be granted options to acquire ordinary shares in the relevant company. The shares must be fully paid up and not redeemable.

The exercise price must be determined by reference to the unrestricted market value of the shares at the date of grant. HMRC may allow companies to determine a market value by reference to date earlier than the date of grant. As for listed companies, the market value can easily be determined but in relation to private companies the market value can be agreed with HMRC in advance.

This is not a statutory requirement but it is good practice for companies to have an agreed market value in case a tax liability arises, which will need to be determined by reference to the market value of the shares at the date of grant.

If the company has more than one class of shares, then the majority of the issued shares of the same class as the class of shares used to grant CSOP options must be either employee-control shares or open market shares. Shares in a company are employee-control shares if the shareholders are able to control the company and those shareholders are employees or directors of the company. Shares in a company are open market shares if they are not held by employees or directors of the company or by their trustees unless they acquired the shares when they were offered to the public.

- **Options** requirement –

The CSOP scheme must state the following terms at the date of grant:

- The exercise price;
- The number and description of shares that may be acquired under the scheme;
- If the shares are restricted securities, the restrictions must be clearly set out in the agreement;
- When the option can be exercised (in whole or in part); and
- If the exercise is subject to performance conditions, the conditions and any circumstances under which the option will lapse or be cancelled (in whole or in part).

Any of the above terms (except for the exercise price) may be varied at any time after the date of grant but the mechanism for any variation must be stated at the time the CSOP option is granted. Any such mechanism must be applied in a way that is fair and reasonable.

Any changes to the share capital of the company may impact on the value of the shares, the subject of the CSOP scheme. Therefore, in certain circumstances the exercise price, the number or description of the shares may be required to be varied accordingly. However, any such variation must ensure that both the value of the shares and the exercise price remain the same before and after the change in the share capital of the company. No such variation can take place if the variation results in any of the requirements for a valid CSOP scheme not being met.

The participant must not transfer his option to any other person. This must be stated in the CSOP scheme and is not subject to any variation.

*When can CSOP options be exercised?*

In order to benefit from the favourable tax treatment, participants must exercise their options on or after the third anniversary of the date of grant but not later than the tenth anniversary of the date of grant. The avoidance of tax or NICs must not be the main purpose or one of the main purposes for the establishment of the scheme.

Performance conditions may be imposed before participants can be allowed to exercise their options. Any such performance conditions must be objective and be determined, together with any mechanism for any future variation, at the date of grant. Any variation to any performance conditions must be fair and reasonable. Otherwise, CSOP options may be exercised early under any of the following circumstances:

- The CSOP scheme may allow participants to exercise their options early in circumstances where a participant ceases to be a qualifying employee by reason of being a good leaver. A participant may be entitled to benefit from the tax reliefs available under the scheme if that participant exercises the options in such circumstances and within six months of becoming a good leaver. However, the relevant company or the scheme organiser may allow participants to exercise the options for any other reason;

- Where the event giving rise to the participant ceasing to be a qualifying employee of the company is the death of the participant, the CSOP scheme may allow the personal representatives of the deceased participant to exercise the options within 12 months of the participant's death whilst preserving any tax benefits. The options lapse if the personal representatives do not exercise the options within 12 months;

- With effect from 17 July 2013 (save for the non-UK company reorganisation arrangement which is effective from 6 April

2014), companies may allow participants to exercise their options within six months or other shorter periods of the following company events:

- a change of control of the company – if as a result of a general offer which is made by a person to existing shareholders of the company, that person obtains control of the CSOP company, options may be exercised within the period of six months after the change of control. However, if an exercise after a change of control results in the shares no longer satisfying the relevant statutory requirements, participants may be allowed to conditionally exercise their options within the period of 20 days before the change of control taking place. That exercise must be stated to be ineffective if the change of control does not take place.

  The company may use its discretion for allowing participants to exercise their options within the 20 days period but any such exercise of their discretion must be applied fairly and reasonably.

  A general offer must be an offer to acquire the whole of the issued share capital of the company or all of the shares of the same class as the CSOP shares. The offer must be made to all of the shareholders on broadly the same terms;

- scheme of arrangement – a scheme of arrangement is a form of change control sanctioned by the court. There is a relatively short period of time in which to exercise the options. An exercise of the options will need to take place after the court authorises the arrangement but before it is sanctioned by the court;

- when a person is bound or otherwise entitled to acquire shares in the company under specific provisions of the Companies Act 2006. In such circumstances, the ability to exercise will be effective once a change of control has taken place;
- non-UK company reorganisation – this is another form of arrangement that may result in a change of control taking place. In such circumstances, participants may be allowed to exercise their options within the period of six months of the occurrence of a non-UK company reorganisation.

The following conditions must be satisfied in relation to any of the above company events taking place, for the exercise of the options by participants to qualify for the relevant tax reliefs:

- The option must be exercised before the third anniversary of the date of grant;
- The participants must receive cash when they dispose of their shares on a change of control;
- The CSOP options must be granted before any offer for a change of control is made;
- The participant is not able to exchange his option for an option in the company that made the general offer;
- The avoidance of tax or NICs must not be the main purpose or one of the main purposes for the establishment of the scheme.

Notifications

Following the grant of CSOP options to qualifying employees, the scheme organiser must notify HMRC. The notification must be done online through the ERS online filing system. The scheme organiser must make the notification by the 6 July following the end of the tax year in which the scheme is implemented.

The notification must be made by that date even if options have not yet been granted under the CSOP scheme. The notification must include a declaration by the scheme organiser that the relevant CSOP statutory provisions in relation to the scheme have been satisfied.

If the scheme organiser grants options to qualifying employees before the first notification is made, the notification must also include a declaration that the relevant CSOP statutory provisions have been satisfied in relation to the scheme and the grant of the options and are still satisfied throughout the period to the notification date.

The scheme organiser is also required to complete online annual returns. All annual returns must be submitted by 6 July after the end of the relevant tax year. The company must notify any changes to the scheme including exercise of options, release or lapse of options, any exchange of options or any other adjustment to any of the CSOP options. The scheme organiser must repeat the declaration of compliance when a change is made to the scheme.

The company must complete the annual return even if there have been no changes that require notification.

*Can the company apply for clearance?*

The scheme organiser is able to apply for advance clearance under the non-statutory advance clearance procedure if the scheme organiser wishes to discuss any elements of the CSOP with HMRC. More particularly, the scheme organiser may wish to discuss any proposed changes to the CSOP or any corporate transactions or otherwise that may have an impact on the validity of the CSOP. The scheme organiser will need to weigh the implications of doing so with the need to ensure that the CSOP remains valid throughout the life of the scheme.

Tax Implications

*For the Company –*

Provided that all relevant requirements are complied with, the company will be entitled to a corporation tax deduction in connection with the CSOP scheme. The company can deduct an amount equal to the benefit obtained by the employee when the options are exercised. This is the most valuable deduction the company can get in connection with the scheme.

The setting up of the scheme is an expense that is specifically allowed as a deductible expense in relation to CSOP schemes provided that no options are granted before the earlier of the date of grant of options under the scheme and the date of declaration by the scheme organiser that the scheme complies with the relevant statutory requirements. However, the day to day operation of the scheme may be deductible under general principles and not under any specific statutory provisions. Such expenses may be claimed in the relevant tax year in which the relevant expense is incurred.

In a group structure, the employee may exercise options to acquire shares in a company which is not the employer of that employee. The corporation tax deduction can only be claimed by the employer company and not by the company in which the employee acquires shares.

The corporation tax deduction can only be claimed in the accounting period in which shares are allotted or transferred to the employee, which, normally, occurs in the accounting period when the exercise of the options takes place.

*For the employee –*

Provided that all relevant conditions, requirements and notifications have been complied with by both the scheme organiser and the participant throughout the life of the scheme or, effectively, until the participant exercise his or her options under the scheme, the following expected tax implications will arise on exercise of the CSOP options.

*On the date of grant?*

There are no tax implications when options are granted to qualifying employees provided that the exercise price is the UMV of the shares on the date of grant. If CSOP options are granted at less than the UMV on the date of grant, the CSOP scheme will lose its approved status and become an unapproved scheme. In such circumstances, the difference between the exercise price and the UMV of the shares on the date of grant will be chargeable to income tax and possibly, NICs. Additional income tax (and, possibly, NICs) may be payable on exercise of the options. This is on the basis that the scheme is unapproved or, in other words, the tax treatment will follow that of an unapproved scheme.

*On exercise?*

Provided that:

- The participant exercises the CSOP options strictly in accordance with the terms of the CSOP scheme;
- The CSOP tax advantaged status is retained throughout the period until the options are exercised or, in other words, all relevant statutory requirements for a valid approved scheme are satisfied throughout that period; and
- There is no tax avoidance motive in the grant or exercise of options under the CSOP scheme,

the exercise of CSOP options will be free from income tax, if the exercise of the CSOP options takes place on the happening of any one of the following events:

- The exercise takes place after the third anniversary of the date of grant and not more than the tenth anniversary of the date of grant;

- The exercise occurs before the third anniversary of the date of grant but as a result of the participant becoming a good leaver. When the participant becomes a good leaver, the participant is able to exercise the options within six months of becoming a good leaver. On the death of the participant, the participant's personal representatives may exercise the participant's CSOP options but not later than 12 months of the death of the participant;

- The exercise occurs before the third anniversary of the date of grant but as a result of any one of the company events referred to above. In brief, the company events are specific events following which a change of control occurs in relation to the relevant company. Participants can exercise within specific times in order to retain any tax benefits.

*Income tax liability?*

If options are exercised in any circumstance other than as described above, income tax may be payable on the difference between the AMV of the shares acquired and the exercise price actually paid by the participant. The income tax implications will be the same as if the participant has exercised an unapproved scheme.

*NICs liability?*

If at the time of exercise of the options, the shares are RCAs, the participant's employer will be required to operate the PAYE system and deduct the income tax due from the participant together with the relevant amount representing Class 1 employee's NICs and also account to HMRC for Class 1 employer's NICs. The shares of listed companies or companies listed on AIM are always RCAs. For this reason, the NICs liability of the employer and the obligation to operate the PAYE system will always apply to those shares.

If an income tax liability arises in connection with the exercise of the shares in circumstances where the employer company is required to operate the PAYE system and deduct the amount of income tax from the participant together with primary Class 1 NICs. The employer will need to pay to HMRC the amount deducted together with the secondary Class 1 NICs. However, the employer may recover its liability in respect of the secondary Class 1 NICs from the participant. It can do so either by way of recovery from the participant or by transferring it to the participant.

*What if the shares are restricted securities?*

With effect from 17 July 2013, CSOP options may be granted to participants over restricted shares. This does not change the fact that the exercise price must represent the UMV of the shares on the date of grant. The shares acquired following exercise of the CSOP options are likely to be restricted securities.

Does this then mean that, in order to avoid the restricted securities regime, the employee needs to consider signing the section 431 election?

Whilst restricted securities can be acquired in circumstances where no income tax liability arises on exercise of CSOP options, it does not mean that the restricted securities regime can simply be ignored.

The participant acquiring restricted securities following an exercise of CSOP options may wish to consider the implications of the restricted securities regime. The participant will have two options:

- Sign the section 431(1) election within 14 days of acquisition so that any benefit received by the participant that represents the difference between the AMV and the UMV is charged to income tax and is payable on acquisition of the restricted securities. In which case any gain on disposal is subject to CGT only; or

- Not sign the election but then any disposal proceeds are multiplied by a percentage that represents the difference between the AMV and the UMV on acquisition and that amount is subject to income tax and possibly NICs on disposal of the shares.

When restricted shares are acquired following exercise of CSOP options, the participant does not need to consider the two options above, as the legislation provides a deeming provision in connection with the section 431(1) election. So effectively, the participant is deemed to have signed the election (more like, a statutory election) and, as a consequence, any gain on disposal of the restricted shares will only be subject to CGT.

However, the legislation also provides that the deeming provision falls away if income tax is payable on exercise of the CSOP options. The obvious solution is, therefore, for the participant to sign the election, in any event, even if the company and the participant are not aware of any issues that may give rise to an income tax liability in connection with the exercise of the CSOP options.

Employers usually insist that employees sign the section 431(1) election on exercise. Whilst the deeming provision is helpful and even useful when no income tax is due on the exercise, often, both companies and employees choose not to rely on that deeming provision.

*On disposal of the shares?*

When the shares are ultimately sold or otherwise disposed of by the participant (now shareholder), either immediately following exercise of the options or after a period of ownership, CGT may be payable on any gain realised by that shareholder. CGT is due if the sale proceeds exceed the price that the participant paid on exercise of the options. The price paid by the participant on exercise is the participant's base cost in the shares. However, any amount on which income tax is paid by the participant together with any liability of the employer to Class 1 NICs that is transferred to the participant is added to the base cost of the shares.

*Will the employee qualify for ER?*

The participant may qualify for ER in respect of the gain provided that the participant can demonstrate compliance with the relevant statutory conditions for the relief in terms of employment and holding of shares in the company for at least two years ending with the date of disposal of the shares.

In addition, and, unlike EMI, the requirement for the holding of at least 5% of the share capital is still relevant to participants acquiring shares in the company under the CSOP scheme. Therefore, if a participant under the CSOP scheme receives options to acquire shares that represent less than 5% of the ordinary share capital of the company, the participant will not be entitled to claim the ER.

## Save As You Earn (SAYE)

A SAYE option scheme is an all employee scheme. This means that participation in the scheme must be offered to all qualifying employees and directors and on similar terms. Participation may be restricted by reference to a qualifying period of service. Such period of service must not exceed five years.

Under the SAYE option scheme, the company grants employees and directors an option to acquire shares in the company. The SAYE option scheme may, as the company wishes, run for a period of three or five years. Depending on the type of scheme, the option may only be exercised after either three or five years from the date of grant. Seven years options were available but abolished with effect from 23 July 2013 so some may still be in existence.

Any grant of options under the SAYE option scheme is conditional on the qualifying employees and directors entering into a savings agreement under which they agree to make payments from salary on a weekly or monthly basis. Such amounts ranging from £5 to £500 per month must be saved and used to acquire shares in the company at the end of the savings period.

As with any other option scheme, the option is risk free to its participants. Other than the payments into a savings account, there is no initial financial commitment on the part of the participants and no obligation to exercise the option in the future. If participants choose not to exercise their options at the end of the savings period or if they wish to cease to participate in the SAYE option scheme at any time before they exercise their options, they may withdraw the savings amount due to them at that time.

*What is the purpose of the SAYE option scheme?*

It is a statutory requirement for a SAYE option scheme to provide benefits to directors and employees in the form of a share option. There must be no other benefit under the scheme and no cash equivalent is allowed. Any cash payment will be treated as a bonus and subject to income tax and NICs in the usual way.

*Which company can set up a SAYE option scheme?*

To qualify, a company must be either listed on a recognised stock exchange or be independent. However, the company is still independent if it is controlled by a corporate trustee of an employee ownership trust.

*Who can participate in a SAYE option scheme?*

- **Employment** requirement –

All employees of the company or of the group must be invited to participate in a SAYE option scheme. The employees can be either full-time or part-time employees. Directors may also participate in the scheme but they have to be full-time directors. HMRC has confirmed that full-time directors must work for the company or the group for at least 25 hours per week.

Participation in the SAYE option scheme may be restricted to employees and full-time directors who have been employed by the company or by a group member for a period not exceeding five years. The company does not have to restrict participation by reference to a qualifying period of time but if it does, it has to be the same to all participants and in any event not more than five years.

Participants must be residents in the UK for tax purposes.

However, the scheme organiser may, at its discretion, wish to invite to a participation in a SAYE option scheme part time directors, employees and directors with less than the qualifying period of service as stated in the scheme rules.

- **Material Interest** requirement –

No! The material interest requirement for SAYE option schemes was removed, subject to transitional provisions, with effect from 13 July 2013.

Other requirements:

- **Shares** requirement –

The participant must be granted options to acquire ordinary shares in the relevant company. The shares must be fully paid up and not redeemable.

The exercise price must be determined by reference to the unrestricted market value of the shares at the date of grant. However, companies may, if they so wish, issue SAYE options at a discount. The discount must not exceed 20% of the market value of the shares at the date of grant. Due to practical reasons, HMRC may allow companies to determine a market value by reference to a date earlier than the date of grant. As for listed companies, the market value can easily be determined but in relation to private companies the market value can be agreed with HMRC in advance.

This is not a statutory requirement but it is good practice for companies to have an agreed market value in case a tax liability arises, which will need to be determined by reference to the market value of the shares at the date of grant.

If the company has more than one class of shares, then the majority of the issued shares of the same class as the class of shares used to grant SAYE options must be either employee-control shares or open market shares. Shares in a company are employee-control shares if the shareholders are able to control the company and those shareholders are employees or directors of the company. Shares in a company are open market shares if they are not held by employees or directors of the company or by their trustees unless they acquired the shares when they were offered to the public.

Any changes to the share capital of the company may impact on the value of the shares, the subject of the SAYE option scheme. Therefore, in certain circumstances the exercise price, the number or description of the shares may be required to be varied accordingly. However, any such variation must ensure that both the value of the shares and the exercise price remain the same before and after the change in the share capital of the company. No such variation can take place if the variation results in any of the requirements for a valid SAYE option scheme not being met.

- **Options** requirement –

The SAYE option scheme must state the following terms at the date of grant:

- The exercise price;
- The number and description of shares that may be acquired under the scheme; and
- If the shares are restricted securities, the restrictions must be clearly set out in the agreement.

The participant must not transfer his or her option to any other person. This must be stated in the SAYE option scheme and is not subject to any variation.

- **Linked savings** requirement –

A SAYE option scheme must be linked to a certified SAYE savings arrangement. A participant is only able to participate in a SAYE option scheme if the participant enters into a contract to make regular contributions for a specified period. That arrangement must be approved by HMRC.

The link between the savings arrangement and the SAYE option scheme is reflected by the fact that, on exercise of the option granted under the scheme, the participant must use the overall value of the savings account of that participant as at the date of exercise to acquire shares in the company. That value reflects the total contributions by the participant during the savings period together with any interest or bonus that the participant may receive from the financial institution that has been contracted by the scheme organiser to operate that savings arrangement. No other funds may be used to acquire shares in the company under the SAYE option scheme.

The number of shares that the participant may acquire can then be calculated by dividing the total value of the savings amount by the exercise price per share.

The scheme organiser may offer a savings arrangement of either three or five years after which options must be exercised. Participants are required to make weekly or monthly contributions into the savings account. The weekly or monthly amount is normally calculated by reference to the amount that the participant requires to pay on exercise of the SAYE option. The monthly amount, or the equivalent weekly amount, must not be less than £5 and not more than £500. The scheme organiser may set a higher minimum amount but it must not exceed £10 per month.

Participants may wish to continue to participate in the SAYE option scheme but take a break from making contributions under the savings arrangement and postpone any additional contributions to a later date. With effect from 1 September 2018, participants may delay the payment of contributions by up to 12 months. Before that date the period was six months.

If a participant fails to make any additional contributions after the 12 months period, the participant will not be able to make any further contributions under that savings arrangement. Except for any special circumstances, referred to below, options may only be exercised after the period in which the participant makes either 36 or 60 monthly contributions into the savings account so an exercise of the option may be delayed following a period of non-payment of the relevant weekly or monthly contributions.

Any such contributions are deducted from the participants' salary. However, in certain circumstances, where such deduction may not be possible, for example, when the participant is on maternity, parental or adoption leave or after cessation of employment the payments can be made by standing order or by any other method directly from the participant to the financial or other institution that manages the savings arrangement.

On cessation of employment, a participant may continue to make monthly contributions for a period of either six months, if the participant wishes to accumulate further amounts with which to exercise at the end of that period, or for the remainder of the 36 or 60 months period, if the participant does not wish to exercise the option but instead wishes to continue to contribute until the maturity of the savings arrangement, as it may include the payment of bonuses and interest.

*When can SAYE options be exercised?*

Participants can exercise their SAYE options within the period of six months after the maturity of the savings arrangement. In other words, within the period of six months after 36 or 60 monthly contributions have been made under the savings arrangement. Exercise of the SAYE options is not normally possible before maturity of the savings arrangement or after the six months period after maturity of the savings arrangement.

An early exercise of the SAYE options is allowed in any one of the following circumstances:

- If a participant dies, the personal representatives of that participant may exercise the SAYE options within the period of 12 months after the death of the participant. An exercise during the

12 months period is allowed in any event where the participant dies either before, on or after the maturity of the savings arrangement;

- If a participant ceases to be employed by the relevant company and that participant is a good lever, the participant is allowed to exercise the SAYE options within the period of six months after the date of cessation of employment. The participant cannot, in any event, exercise the SAYE options after the six months period after either cessation of employment or maturity of the savings arrangement. Therefore, if cessation of employment occurs after the maturity of the relevant savings arrangement, the participant can only exercise by the end of the six months period after maturity of the savings arrangement. The scheme rules must allow participants to exercise in such circumstances;

- Companies may allow participants to exercise their options within six months of the following company events:

    - a change of control of the company – if as a result of a general offer which is made by a person to existing shareholders of the company, that person obtains control of the SAYE company, options may be exercised within the period of six months after the change of control. A general offer must be an offer to acquire the whole of the issued share capital of the company or all of the shares of the same class as the SAYE shares. The offer must be made to all of the shareholders on broadly the same terms;

    - scheme of arrangement – a scheme of arrangement is a form of change control sanctioned by the court. There is a relatively short period of time in which to exercise the options. An exercise of the options will need to take place after the court authorises the arrangement but before it is sanctioned by the court;

- when a person is bound or otherwise entitled to acquire shares in the company under specific provisions of the Companies Act 2006. In such circumstances, the ability to exercise will be effective once a change of control has taken place;

- the company passes a resolution for the voluntary winding up of the company;

- non-UK company reorganisation – this is another form of arrangement that may result in a change of control taking place. In such circumstances, participants may be allowed to exercise their options within the period of six months of the occurrence of a non-UK company reorganisation.

However, if an exercise after a change of control results in the shares no longer satisfying the relevant statutory requirements for a valid SAYE option scheme, participants may normally be allowed to exercise their options within the following periods:

- Participants may be allowed to conditionally exercise their options within the period of 20 days before the change of control taking place. That exercise must be stated to be ineffective if the change of control does not take place;

- Participants may be allowed to exercise their options within the period of 20 days after the relevant change of control taking place.

In any event, options cannot be exercised after the period of six months after the maturity of the relevant savings arrangement.

The company may use its discretion for allowing participants to exercise their options within the 20 days period but any such exercise of their discretion must be applied fairly and reasonably.

Scheme rules may include provisions allowing participants to exchange their SAYE options with SAYE options in the acquiring company following a change of control. Participants may not be offered replacement SAYE options in the acquiring company in which case, participants can exercise their options on a change of control instead. However, if replacement options are offered:

- The value of the shares and the exercise price must be substantially the same as before the change of control;
- The options must be capable of being exercised as before, i.e. within the period of six months after maturity of the relevant savings arrangement; and
- The relevant requirements for a valid SAYE option scheme must be satisfied by the acquiring company.

Notifications

Following the grant of SAYE options to employees of the company, the scheme organiser must notify HMRC. The notification must be done online through the ERS online filing system. The scheme organiser must make the notification by the 6 July following the end of the tax year in which the scheme is implemented.

The notification must be made by that date even if options have not yet been granted under the SAYE option scheme. The notification must include a declaration by the scheme organiser that the relevant SAYE statutory requirements in relation to the scheme have been satisfied.

If the scheme organiser grants options to qualifying employees before the first notification is made, the notification must also include a declaration that the relevant SAYE statutory provisions have been satisfied in relation to the scheme and the grant of the options and are still satisfied throughout the period to the notification date.

The scheme organiser is also required to complete online annual returns. All annual returns must be submitted by 6 July after the end of the relevant tax year. The company must notify any changes to the scheme including exercise of options, release or lapse of options, any exchange of options or any other adjustment to any of the SAYE options. The scheme organiser must repeat the declaration of compliance when a change is made to the scheme.

The company must complete the annual return even if there have been no changes that require notification.

*Can the company apply for clearance?*

The scheme organiser is able to apply for advance clearance under the non-statutory advance clearance procedure if the scheme organiser wishes to discuss any elements of the SAYE option scheme with HMRC. More particularly, the scheme organiser may wish to discuss any proposed changes to the SAYE option scheme or any corporate transactions or otherwise that may have an impact on the validity of the SAYE option scheme. The scheme organiser will need to weigh the implications of doing so with the need to ensure that the SAYE option scheme remains valid throughout the life of the scheme.

<u>Tax Implications</u>

*For the Company –*

Provided that all relevant requirements are complied with, the company will be entitled to a corporation tax deduction in connection with the CSOP scheme. The company can deduct an amount equal to the benefit obtained by the employee when the options are exercised. This is the most valuable deduction the company can get in connection with the scheme.

The setting up of the scheme is an expense that is specifically allowed as a deductible expense in relation to SAYE option schemes provided that no options are granted before the earlier of the date of grant of options under the scheme and the date of declaration by the scheme organiser that the scheme complies with the relevant statutory requirements. However, the day to day operation of the scheme may be deductible under general principles and not under any specific statutory provisions. Such expenses may be claimed in the relevant tax year in which the relevant expense is incurred.

In a group structure, the employee may exercise options to acquire shares in a company which is not the employer of that employee. The corporation tax deduction can only be claimed by the employer company and not by the company in which the employee acquires shares.

The corporation tax deduction can only be claimed in the accounting period in which shares are allotted or transferred to the employee, which, normally, occurs in the accounting period when the exercise of the options takes place.

*For the employee –*

Provided that all relevant conditions, requirements and notifications have been complied with by both the scheme organiser and the participant throughout the life of the scheme or, effectively, until the participant exercise his or her options under the scheme, the following expected tax implications will arise on exercise of the SAYE options.

*On the date of grant?*

There are no tax implications when options are granted to qualifying employees.

*On exercise?*

Provided that:

- The participant exercises the SAYE options strictly in accordance with the terms of the SAYE option scheme;

- The SAYE tax advantaged status is retained throughout the period until the options are exercised or, in other words, all relevant statutory requirements for a valid approved scheme are satisfied throughout that period; and

- There is no tax avoidance motive in the grant or exercise of options under the SAYE option scheme,

the exercise of SAYE options will be free from income tax, if the exercise of the SAYE options takes place on the happening of any one of the following events:

- The exercise takes place on or after the third anniversary of the date of grant;

- The exercise occurs before the third anniversary of the date of grant but as a result of the participant becoming a good leaver. When the participant becomes a good leaver, the participant is able to exercise the options within six months of becoming a good leaver. On the death of the participant, the participant's personal representatives may exercise the participant's SAYE options but not later than 12 months of the death of the participant;

- The exercise occurs before the third anniversary of the date of grant but as a result of any one of the company events referred to above. In brief, the company events are specific events following which a change of control occurs in relation to the relevant company. Participants can exercise within specific times in order to retain any tax benefits.

*Income tax liability?*

If options are exercised in any circumstance other than as described above, income tax may be payable on the difference between the AMV of the shares acquired and the exercise price actually paid by the participant. The income tax implications will be the same as if the participant has exercised an unapproved scheme.

*NICs liability?*

Shares used for the purpose of a SAYE option scheme are not RCAs. Therefore, if income tax becomes payable following the exercise of the SAYE options, the participant will be required to complete a self-assessment tax return and pay the income tax due by the 31 January after the end of the relevant tax year in which the income tax liability arises. As the SAYE shares are not RCAs, the income tax liability will not attract any liability to pay NICs. HMRC allows employers to deduct the income tax liability from the participants' salary and pay it over to HMRC if participants do not normally file self-assessment tax returns.

However, the participant's employer may still be required to operate the PAYE system and deduct the income tax due from the participant together with the relevant amount representing Class 1 employee's NICs and also account to HMRC for Class 1 employer's NICs in circumstances where options are not exercised in accordance with the scheme rules.

If an income tax liability arises in connection with the exercise of the shares in circumstances where the employer company is required to operate the PAYE system and deduct the amount of income tax from the participant together with primary Class 1 NICs. The employer will need to pay to HMRC the amount deducted together with the secondary Class 1 NICs. However, the employer may recover its liability in respect of the secondary Class 1 NICs from the participant. It can do so either by way of recovery from the participant or by transferring it to the participant. The shares of listed companies or companies listed on AIM are always RCAs. For this reason, the NICs liability of the employer and the obligation to operate the PAYE system will always apply to those shares.

By statute, any interest, which, includes any bonuses, that the participants receive from the relevant financial institution in respect of their contributions under the savings arrangement is not subject to income tax.

*What if the shares are restricted securities?*

Whilst SAYE options may be granted to participants over restricted shares, the exercise price must nonetheless represent not less than 80% of the UMV of the shares on the date of grant. The shares acquired following exercise of the SAYE options are likely to be restricted securities in any event. Does this then mean that, in order to avoid the restricted securities regime, the participant needs to consider signing the section 431(1) election?

Whilst restricted securities can be acquired in circumstances where no income tax liability arises on exercise of SAYE options, it does not mean that the restricted securities regime can simply be ignored.

The participant acquiring restricted securities following an exercise of SAYE options may wish to consider the implications of the restricted securities regime. The participant will have two options:

- Sign the section 431(1) election within 14 days of acquisition so that any benefit received by the participant that represents the difference between the AMV and the UMV is charged to income tax and is payable on acquisition of the restricted securities. In which case any gain on disposal is subject to CGT only; or

- Not sign the election but then any disposal proceeds are multiplied by a percentage that represents the difference between the AMV and the UMV on acquisition and that amount is subject to income tax and possibly NICs on disposal of the shares.

When restricted shares are acquired following exercise of SAYE options, the participant does not need to consider the two options above, as the legislation provides a deeming provision in connection with the section 431(1) election. So effectively, the participant is deemed to have signed the election and, as a consequence, any gain on disposal of the restricted shares will only be subject to CGT.

However, the legislation also provides that the deeming provision falls away if income tax is payable on exercise of the SAYE options. The obvious solution is, therefore, for the participant to sign the election, in any event, even if the company and the participant are not aware of any issues that may give rise to an income tax liability in connection with the exercise of the SAYE options.

Employers usually insist that employees sign the section 431(1) election on exercise. Whilst the deeming provision is helpful and even useful when no income tax is due on the exercise, often, both companies and employees choose not to rely on that deeming provision.

*On disposal of the shares?*

When the shares are ultimately sold or otherwise disposed of by the participant (now shareholder), either immediately following exercise of the options or after a period of ownership, CGT may be payable on any gain realised by that shareholder. CGT is due if the sale proceeds exceed the price that the participant paid on exercise of the options. The price paid by the participant on exercise is the participant's base cost in the shares. However, any amount on which income tax is paid by the participant together with any liability of the employer to Class 1 NICs that is transferred to the participant is added to the base cost of the shares.

*Will the employee qualify for ER?*

The employee may qualify for ER in respect of the gain provided that the employee can demonstrate compliance with the relevant statutory conditions for the relief in terms of employment and holding of shares in the company for at least two years ending with the date of disposal of the shares.

In addition, the employee will need to comply with the requirement for the holding of at least 5% of the share capital of the company. It is very highly unlikely that employees receive 5% or more of the ordinary share capital of the company under the SAYE option scheme so will most probably not be entitled to ER.

## Share Incentive Plan (SIP)

Unlike any of the other approved schemes, A SIP is not an option scheme. it is a scheme that enables employees to receive or acquire shares in the company from the word go. However, the shares are not held by employees but by a UK resident Employee Benefit Trust (EBT).

One of the only similarities that a SIP has with the SAYE option scheme is that the SIP is also an all employee scheme. This means that participation in the scheme must be offered to all qualifying employees and directors and on similar terms. Participation may be restricted by reference to a qualifying period of service. Such period of service must not exceed 18 months.

There are four types of awards in a typical SIP. More on which below. They are:

- Free shares – participants receive free shares from the company;
- Partnership shares – participants are invited to acquire further shares from the company;
- Matching shares – participants receive additional free shares from the company; and
- Dividend shares – participants reinvest any cash dividends in acquiring additional shares in the company.

There is no obligation for all four types to be included within a SIP. A scheme organiser can, therefore, have a choice as to the award that can be included.

Provided that all relevant requirements in relation to a valid scheme are satisfied, employees can expect to receive tax free awards under the SIP if shares are held by the UK EBT trustees for a period of three to five years.

*What is the purpose of the SIP?*

It is a statutory requirement for a SIP to provide benefits to employees in the form of shares in the company which give them continuing stake in the company. There must be no other benefit under the scheme and no cash equivalent is allowed. Any cash payment will be treated as a bonus and subject to income tax and NICs in the usual way.

General requirements:

Being an all employee plan, the SIP must not contain within it any features that has or is likely to have the effect of discouraging any of the employees from participating in the SIP. HMRC provides examples of such discouraging features as:

- A provision in the plan that requires employees to acquire shares in the company outside the SIP as a condition for participation in the SIP;

- Invitations to participation in the SIP must be advertised for not less than 14 days, as some employees may be absent for a shorter period of time and may miss the opportunity to participate;

- Employees should be able to opt out of an award of shares if they so wish. A period of 25 days is considered sufficient for employees to consider their options and seek professional advice if they so required. All employees must be invited to participate in any award the company offer even if they opt out of another award;

- Invitations must not be aimed at specific groups of employees but to all employees on similar terms;

All employees who are qualifying employees must be able to participate on the same terms. However, companies are allowed to award free shares by reference to:

- An employee's remuneration;
- An employee's length of service; or
- Hours worked by the employee.

Companies can apply these factors separately but not together. For example, the company may determine the number of free shares to be awarded by reference to the employee's length of service but the company cannot use both length of service and hours worked in determining the number of shares.

The company must not give preferential treatment to directors and senior employees receiving the highest level of remuneration and in group structures, directors and senior employees of specific members of the group.

The SIP must not contain any conditions on participation that are not required or authorised by the relevant statutory provisions for a valid SIP. HMRC provides three examples to such conditions:

- A rule that prevents employees from participation if they had already received cash bonuses or other benefits. The rule does not have to be contained in the SIP;
- A condition preventing employees from participation if they have participated in the SIP before;
- Limiting participation to employees of a recently acquired subsidiary.

Any arrangement in respect of employees' participation in the company's SIP must not include the making of any loans to any of the employees.

*Which company can set up a SIP?*

To qualify, a company must be either listed on a recognised stock exchange or be independent. However, the company is still independent if it is controlled by a corporate trustee of an employee ownership trust.

A service company or a company that controls the service company cannot set up a SIP. A service company is a company that provides the services of employees employed by it to people who control it.

*Who can participate in a SIP?*

- **Employment** requirement –

The employee must be UK resident for tax purposes and an employee of the company or, in group structures, the employee must be an employee of a constituent company. Non-UK residents may be invited to participate in the SIP.

If the SIP requires an employee to work for the relevant company for a qualifying period of time before that employee can participate in the SIP, the employee must work for the relevant qualifying company throughout that period.

If the SIP includes a qualifying period of time, it must not exceed:

- In the case of free shares, the period of 18 months ending with the date on which the award of free shares is made;
- In the case of partnership shares with no accumulation period, the period of 18 months ending with the date on which the deduction from the employee's salary is made;

- In the case of partnership shares with accumulation period, the period of six months ending with the start of the accumulation period relating to the award;

- In the case of matching shares with no accumulation period, the period of 18 months ending with the date on which the deduction from the employee's salary is made for the partnership shares to which the matching shares relate;

- In the case of matching shares with accumulation period, the period of six months ending with the start of the accumulation period relating to the partnership shares to which the matching shares relate.

The company may use different qualifying periods in respect of different awards of shares but the above rules must apply to any such qualifying period of time. In any event, any such qualifying periods of time must apply to all employees of the company or constituent company.

An accumulation period is a period of not more than one year, in which deductions from salary are made and used to acquire partnership shares and matching shares. As the market value of the shares acquired by employees under the SIP is determined by reference to the date on which shares are acquired, a SIP with or without an accumulation period may impact on the value of the shares acquired.

An employee may participate in a SIP if the employee is an eligible employee at the appropriate time:

- In the case of free shares, the time when the award is made;

- In the case of partnership shares with no accumulation period, the time when the deduction from the employee's salary is made;

- In the case of partnership shares with accumulation period, the time of the first deduction relating to the award;
- In the case of matching shares with no accumulation period, the time a deduction from the employee's salary is made for the partnership shares to which the matching shares relate;
- In the case of matching shares with accumulation period, the time of the first deduction relating to the partnership shares to which the matching shares relate.

Employees cannot participate in more than one SIP of connected companies at the same time in the same tax year. However, they may join consecutive ones in the same tax year.

- **Shares** requirement –

Eligible shares must form the ordinary share capital of the company, a company which has control of the company or a company which either is, or has control of, a company which is a member of a consortium owning either the company or a company that controls the company. The shares must be fully paid up and not redeemable.

The four awards:

- Free shares –

If a company chooses to award eligible employees with free shares, the company can award up to a maximum of £3,600 worth of free shares per tax year per employee. The value of the shares is determined by reference to the UMV of the shares on the date of the award.

The company must set a holding period in respect of which free shares must be held by the SIP trustees as legal owners on behalf of eligible employees who have the beneficial ownership in the shares. Eligible employees must not assign, transfer or otherwise dispose of their beneficial interest in the shares. The holding period must be at least three years but not more than five years. The holding period can be set by the company as any period between three and five years but any such period must apply to all free shares within the same award.

If a participant ceases to be an employee of the company during the holding period, the shares can no longer be subject to the SIP and must be removed out of the trust. In such circumstances, the plan rules may specify that the shares must be forfeited and the participant will lose the beneficial ownership in the shares. Otherwise, shares can be transferred to the participant.

The award can be linked to performance which must apply to all qualifying employees. The performance targets can be used to determine whether or not employees receive free shares and to the extent they do, the number and value of shares. The company must notify all eligible employees of any performance targets and measures as soon as reasonably practicable.

- Partnership Shares –

The SIP may allow eligible employees to acquire shares from the company. The shares are called partnership shares. An eligible employee must enter into a partnership share agreement with the company under which the employee authorises the employer company to deduct part of the employee's salary for the purpose of the acquisition of partnership shares in the company.

The partnership share agreement must include information about the amounts that the employer company can deduct from the employee's salary and how often. The employee and the company may later agree between them to change the amounts to be deducted and the number of deductions but in any event any such deductions must not exceed the maximum amount that can be deducted for the purchase of partnership shares.

The maximum amount that can be deducted from an employee's salary for any tax year must not exceed the lesser of £1,800 and 10% of the employee's salary for that tax year. For example, if an employee receives a salary of £25,000 per year, the maximum amount that can be deducted for the purpose of the purchase of partnership shares is £1,800. If an employee receives a salary of £15,000 per year, the maximum amount is £1,500.

The company may specify lower limits than the limits specified above. Different limits may apply to different awards of partnership shares as long as those limits do not exceed the lesser of £1,800 and 10% of the employee's salary per tax year. The SIP may specify a minimum amount to be deducted on any occasion. The minimum amount must not be greater than £10.

The deduction is made from gross salary before tax. The partnership share agreement must contain a notice under which employees are informed of the possible impact that any such deduction may have on the employee's entitlement to social security benefits, statutory sick pay and statutory maternity pay. Such benefits are calculated by reference to the gross salary of the employee. However, a deduction for the purchase of partnership shares reduces the amount of gross salary and as a consequence any benefits that the employee may be entitled to receive in respect of social security, statutory sick and maternity pay.

The employer company must pay any amount deducted from the employee's salary to the SIP trustees as soon as practicable. The SIP trustees must hold the amount deducted on behalf of the relevant employee until such time as the money is applied in acquiring partnership shares on the employee's behalf. The SIP trustees must account to the employee for any interest if the money is held on behalf of the employee in an interest-bearing account.

*Accumulation period not included?*

If the SIP does not provide for an accumulation period, the money deducted from the employee's salary must be applied by the trustees in acquiring partnership shares on behalf of the employee. Partnership shares must be acquired not later than 30 days after the last date on the money was deducted. The number of partnership shares to be acquired on behalf of the employee must be determined by reference to the market value of the shares on the acquisition date. If any amount remains after the acquisition of partnership shares, the employee may agree with the SIP trustees to either carry forward any surplus amount and add it to the amount of the next deduction or pay it back to the employee as soon as practicable. If any amount is paid back to the employee, it is paid subject to deduction of income tax and NICs under the PAYE system, as the money was originally deducted from gross salary before deduction of tax.

*Accumulation period included?*

If the SIP provides for an accumulation period, the accumulation period must not exceed 12 months. The partnership share agreement must specify the period from which the accumulation period commences and ends. The accumulation period must begin with the first deduction from salary and, in relation to each award of partnership shares, must be the same for all employees entering into the partnership share agreements.

The accumulated amount of money deducted from the employee's salary over the accumulation period must be applied by the SIP trustees in acquiring partnership shares on behalf of the employee not later than 30 days after the end of the accumulation period. The number of shares to be acquired are determined by reference to any one of the following methods, which method must be specified in the partnership share agreement:

- The lower of the market value of the shares at the beginning of the accumulation period and the market value of the shares on the acquisition date;
- The market value of the shares at the beginning of the accumulation period; or

- The market value of the shares on the acquisition date.

As with a SIP that does not provide for an accumulation period, if any amount remains after the acquisition of partnership shares, the employee may agree with the SIP trustees to either carry forward any surplus amount and add it to the amount of the next accumulation period or pay it back to the employee as soon as practicable. If an employee ceases to be an employee of the relevant company during the accumulation period, any deducted amount must be paid over to that employee as soon as practicable. Again, if any amount is paid back to the employee, it is paid subject to deduction of income tax and NICs under the PAYE system, as the money was originally deducted from gross salary before deduction of tax.

The company may limit the number of partnership shares that may be acquired by the trustees on behalf of employees. The company may specify different maximum number of shares in respect of different awards. In any case, the company must notify the employees of any restriction on the number of partnership shares that may be acquired under any particular award. The notification by the company must be made before the first deduction is made when the SIP does not provide for an accumulation period and, before the beginning of the accumulation period if the SIP provides for an accumulation period.

Subject to certain conditions relating to the employee's ability to restart any additional deductions, employees are permitted to require the company to stop any deductions from salary for the purpose of the partnership share agreement. An employee is also permitted to withdraw from the partnership share agreement altogether by notifying the company of the employee's intention. Save in circumstances where the employee wishes to continue to make deductions in connection with the accumulation period at a later date, any amounts held by the SIP trustees must be paid over to the employee as soon as practicable but subject to deduction of income tax and NICs under the PAYE system.

Once partnership shares have been acquired on behalf of an employee, the employee may, at any time, withdraw all or part of the partnership shares from the SIP. However, depending on the timing of the withdrawal of the shares from the SIP, such withdrawal, if not in accordance with the SIP rules, may be subject to tax on any benefit received by the employee.

Partnership shares cannot be forfeited at the direction of either the company or the SIP trustees. However, partnership shares may be subject to a requirement whereby they can be offered for sale if the employee ceases to be an employee of the relevant company. The employee must receive a consideration, for the sale of the partnership shares, equal to the lower of the amount paid by the employee in acquiring the partnership shares and the market value of the shares at the time they are offered for sale.

In order to retain all the tax benefits under the SIP, partnership shares must be held by the UK EBT trustees for a period of three to five years.

- Matching shares –

If the SIP includes the award of partnership shares whereby shares can be acquired by the SIP trustees on behalf of the employees, the company may also choose to award employees with matching shares. The award of matching shares can be included within the partnership share agreement. The matching shares must be shares of the same class and must carry the same rights as the partnership shares to which the matching shares relate. They must be awarded to employees on the same day as the partnership shares and must be awarded to all employees on exactly the same basis.

The company can offer a number of additional free shares to match the acquisition of partnership shares by employees. The ratio must not exceed 2:1 or, in other words, two matching shares for every one partnership share. For as long as the company does not offer more than two matching shares for every one partnership share, the company can you use any combination. For example, the company may offer one matching share for every two partnership shares and so on.

The partnership share agreement must specify the ratio offered by the company and, if the company wishes to change that ratio, the circumstances and the way that ratio may be changed. The company must inform the employees of any change before partnership shares are awarded under the partnership share agreement.

In order to retain all the tax benefits under the SIP, matching shares must be held by the UK EBT trustees for a period of three to five years.

- Dividend shares –

Once participants in a SIP receive free shares and perhaps acquire additional partnership shares and even receive more free matching shares from the company, they may be entitled to receive dividends on those shares. They would normally have a choice as to whether they wish to take the cash dividend and, subject to the payment of tax on the cash dividend, spend it as they please or use the cash dividend to reinvest it in the acquisition of additional shares in the company. The additional shares acquired from the participants' entitlement to cash dividends are called dividend shares.

The SIP may otherwise direct that the SIP trustees must apply any cash dividends in acquiring additional dividend shares on behalf of either all participants or all participants who opt to reinvest their cash dividends in the acquisition of additional shares. The company is allowed to take whatever course it wishes in relation to the reinvestment of cash dividends.

The company must specify how much of the cash dividends can be reinvested and can modify or revoke any direction in connection with the reinvestment of cash dividends. With effect from 6 April 2013, the reinvestment is not subject to any limits, either monetary or timing of reinvestment.

If the SIP allows for the reinvestment of cash dividends, the SIP must specify that dividend shares must be shares of the same class and must carry the same rights as the shares in respect of which the dividend is paid.

The dividend shares must not be subject to any provision for forfeiture at the direction of either the company or the SIP trustees. However, dividend shares shares may be subject to a requirement whereby they can be offered for sale if the employee ceases to be an employee of the relevant company. If the shares are offered for sale, the employee must receive a consideration, for the sale of the dividends shares, equal to the lower of the amount of the original cash dividends used by the SIP trustees to acquire dividend shares on behalf of the employee and the market value of the shares at the time they are offered for sale.

The SIP must also specify that the SIP trustees must treat all participants, who reinvest cash dividends in the acquisition of dividend shares, fairly and equally in connection with the reinvestment. Dividend shares must be acquired by the SIP trustees on behalf of participants on a date to be determined by the SIP trustees but not later than 30 days after the dividends is received by them. The number of dividend shares is determined by reference to the market value of the shares at the time they acquired by the SIP trustees.

The holding period in respect of which dividend shares must be held by the SIP trustees as legal owners on behalf of eligible employees who have the beneficial ownership in the shares is three years. Eligible employees must not assign, transfer or otherwise dispose of their beneficial interest in the shares.

If a participant ceases to be an employee of the company during the holding period, the shares can no longer be subject to the SIP and must be removed out of the trust. In such circumstances, shares can be transferred to the participant or sold subject to the employee receiving a consideration, for the sale of the dividends shares, equal to the lower of the amount of the original cash dividends used by the SIP trustees to acquire dividend shares on behalf of the employee and the market value of the shares at the time they are offered for sale.

Any surplus cash dividend that is not sufficient to acquire dividend shares may be left with the SIP trustees and added to the next cash dividends received by the SIP trustees. If participants cease to be employees of the company or the SIP is terminated, the SIP trustees must transfer any surplus cash dividend to the participants as soon as practicable. In circumstances where cash dividends are not reinvested in the acquisition of dividend shares, any cash dividend must be paid over to participants as soon as practicable.

Any amount of cash dividends paid to participants whether in respect of any surplus or the full amount when it is not used to acquire dividends shares, is subject to tax which is calculated by reference to the dividend rate in the tax year in which the money is paid to the participant and not when the cash dividend arose. The tax is paid by the participant by completing a self-assessment tax return by the 31 January after the end of the relevant tax year.

Disqualifying event

With effect from 15 September 2016, the SIP will cease to be a valid SIP if a disqualifying event occurs.

*What are the disqualifying events?*

- Any alteration to the company's share capital or the rights attaching to any of the shares, the subject of the SIP that materially affects the value of the shares, the subject of the SIP;

- SIP shares receive different treatment than shares of the same class. Particularly, in respect of the dividend payable, any repayment of capital or any offer of substituted or additional shares, securities or rights of any description in respect of the shares.

*Not a disqualifying event?*

SIP shares receiving a different treatment as a result of:

- A key feature of the SIP or, in other words, a key feature or provision that is required in order to ensure that the statutory requirements of the SIP are, at all times, met;
- Any restrictions that apply to the participants' shares; or
- Newly issued SIP shares receiving a different treatment, in respect of dividends payable before the date of issue of the SIP shares, than shares issued before that date.

*What is the effect of the disqualifying event?*

The tax treatment of any shares awarded to participants under the SIP will not be affected provided that they are awarded to participants before the occurrence of the disqualifying event. The tax treatment will be affected after that date.

Valuation

Shares in the company need to be valued for the purpose of any share scheme or otherwise in respect of any transaction in shares. Valuation of the shares is not a statutory requirement but is highly recommended in any event.

Valuation of the shares helps determine the value of the shares of the purpose of the individual limits and is necessary to determine the income tax liability of the employee if the shares or any part of them become subject to income tax either on any benefit received by employees or by reference to the restricted securities regime.

As for listed companies, the market value can easily be determined but in relation to private companies the market value can be agreed with HMRC in advance.

Notifications

Following the set-up of a SIP, the company must notify HMRC. The notification must be done online through the ERS online filing system. The company must make the notification by the 6 July following the end of the tax year in which the SIP is implemented.

The notification must include a declaration by the company that the relevant statutory requirements in relation to the SIP have been satisfied.

If the company awards free shares to qualifying employees before the first notification is made, the notification must also include a declaration that the relevant statutory provisions have been satisfied in relation to the SIP and the award of shares and are still satisfied throughout the period to the notification date.

The company is also required to complete online annual returns. All annual returns must be submitted by 6 July after the end of the relevant tax year. The company must notify any changes to the SIP. The company must repeat the declaration of compliance when a change is made to the SIP.

The company must complete the annual return even if there have been no changes that require notification.

*Can the company apply for clearance?*

The scheme organiser is able to apply for advance clearance under the non-statutory advance clearance procedure if the scheme organiser wishes to discuss any elements of the SIP with HMRC. More particularly, the scheme organiser may wish to discuss any proposed changes to the SIP or any corporate transactions or otherwise that may have an impact on the validity of the SIP. The scheme organiser will need to weigh the implications of doing so with the need to ensure that the SIP remains valid throughout the life of the SIP.

## Tax Implications

*For the employer Company –*

Provided that all relevant requirements are complied with, the employer company will be entitled to a corporation tax deduction in connection with the award of free and matching shares. The company can deduct an amount equal to the market value of the free and matching shares as at the date the award is made.

In regard to partnership shares, the employer company is entitled to a corporation tax deduction under general principles in respect of the amount of salary that the employee uses in order to acquire partnership shares. If the market value of the shares, on the acquisition date of the partnership shares, exceeds the value paid by the employees, the excess amount can also be used by the employer company as a corporation tax deduction.

There is no corporation tax deduction in connection with dividend shares.

If the employer company wishes to get a deduction for the amounts spent on setting up the scheme and the operation of the scheme throughout its life, the company may need to rely on either specific statutory provisions or under general principles but such expenses are generally allowed.

However, corporation tax deduction is not possible if the participant is not resident in the UK at the time of the award or if the shares that have been forfeited by the relevant employee.

*For the SIP Trustees –*

Subject to conditions, the SIP trustees are also entitled to specific statutory tax reliefs in respect of any cash dividends they receive in respect of any shares not held on behalf of any employee and any CGT on the rise of value of shares that they hold and that are not awarded to employees.

*For the employee –*

Provided that all relevant conditions, requirements and notifications have been complied with by both the scheme organiser and the participant throughout the life of the SIP, the following expected tax implications will arise.

*On the award of free and matching shares?*

There are no income tax implications when free or matching shares are awarded to qualifying employees. There is no stamp duty on the transfer to participants of free or matching shares by the SIP trustees or when participants are issued new shares in the company.

*On the acquisition of partnership shares?*

There are no income tax implications when partnership shares are acquired by qualifying employees. The amount of salary used for the purpose of acquiring the partnership shares is not subject to tax under the PAYE system or otherwise. There is no stamp duty on the transfer to participants of partnership shares by the SIP trustees.

*On the acquisition of dividend shares?*

There are no income tax implications when dividend shares are acquired by qualifying employees. The cash dividends held by the SIP trustees on behalf of employees for reinvestment in the acquisition of dividend shares are not subject to income tax at the dividend rate. There is no stamp duty on the transfer to participants of dividend shares by the SIP trustees.

*On expiration of the five years holding period or the occurrence of other events?*

Provided that:

- Free, Partnership and matching shares, if relevant, are held by the SIP trustees for the required holding period of five years and in relation to dividend shares, three years;
- The SIP tax advantaged status is retained throughout the period until the end of the relevant holding period or, in other words, all relevant statutory requirements for a valid approved scheme are satisfied throughout that period; and
- There is no tax avoidance motive in the award or acquisition of shares under the SIP,

shares awarded to, or acquired by, participants will be free from income tax on the happening of any one of the following events:

- The shares remain in the SIP trust until the expiration of the relevant holding period on or after the fifth or third anniversary of the date the award or acquisition of shares is made;
- The shares are withdrawn from the SIP trust before the end of the relevant holding period of the date the award or acquisition of shares is made as a result of the participant becoming a good leaver;
- The shares are withdrawn from the SIP trust before the end of the relevant holding period of the date the award or acquisition of shares is made as a result of any one of the corporate events.

The corporate events are:

- A change of control of the company – if as a result of a general offer which is made by a person to existing shareholders of the company, that person obtains control of the company. A general offer must be an offer to acquire the whole of the issued share capital of the company or all of the shares of the same class as the SIP shares. The offer must be made to all of the shareholders on broadly the same terms;

- Scheme of arrangement – a scheme of arrangement is a form of change control sanctioned by the court;

- When a person is bound or otherwise entitled to acquire shares in the company under specific provisions of the Companies Act 2006;

- The company passes a resolution for the voluntary winding up of the company;

- Non-UK company reorganisation – this is another form of arrangement that may result in a change of control taking place.

*Income tax liability?*

If shares are withdrawn from the SIP trust before the fifth anniversary of the date the award or acquisition of shares is made or in any circumstance other than as described above, income tax may be payable as follows:

*Withdrawal of free and matching shares?*

- Shares withdrawn during first three years –

Income tax is payable on the market value of the shares on the date the shares are withdrawn from the SIP trust.

- Shares withdrawn in the period between three and five years –

Income tax is payable on the lower of the market value of the shares on the award date and the market value of the shares on the date the shares are withdrawn from the SIP trust.

*Withdrawal of partnership shares?*

- Shares withdrawn during first three years –

Income tax is payable on the market value of the shares on the date the shares are withdrawn from the SIP trust. However, if the participant is required under the terms of the SIP to offer the shares for sale the income tax liability will be the lower of the UMV of the shares on the date they are offered for sale and the amount of the partnership money used to acquire the shares.

- Shares withdrawn in the period between three and five years –

Income tax is payable on the lower of the market value of the shares on the date the shares are withdrawn from the SIP trust but if the participant is required under the terms of the SIP to offer the shares for sale, the UMV of the shares on the date they are offered for sale and the amount of the partnership money used to acquire the shares.

*Withdrawal of dividend shares?*

- Shares withdrawn during first three years –

Income tax is payable, at the dividend rate, on the cash dividend used to acquire the dividend shares. However, if the participant is required under the terms of the SIP to offer the shares for sale, the income tax liability will be the lower of the UMV of the shares on the date they are offered for sale and the amount of the cash dividend used to acquire the dividend shares.

The income tax is payable in the tax year in which the money is paid to the participant and not when the cash dividend arose. The tax is paid by the participant by completing a self-assessment tax return by the 31 January after the end of the relevant tax year.

*NICs liability?*

If an income tax liability arises by reason of any payment of partnership money back to the employee, the payment will be subject to an obligation on the employer to operate the PAYE system in relation to it. The obligation to operate the PAYE system includes the obligation to deduct an amount in respect of NICs both employee and employer. Otherwise, if shares are withdrawn from the SIP trust in circumstances where an income tax liability arises, the participant's employer will be required to operate the PAYE system and deduct the income tax due from the participant together with the relevant amount representing Class 1 employee's NICs and also account to HMRC for Class 1 employer's NICs if the shares are RCAs.

The shares of listed companies or companies listed on AIM are always RCAs. For this reason, the NICs liability of the employer and the obligation to operate the PAYE system will always apply to those shares.

*What if the shares are restricted securities?*

Whilst SIP shares may be awarded to, or acquired by, participants over restricted shares, the value of the shares must nonetheless represent the UMV of the shares on the date the award is made or the acquisition date.

Whilst restricted securities can be acquired in circumstances where no income tax liability arises, it does not mean that the restricted securities regime can simply be ignored.

The participant may wish to consider the implications of the restricted securities regime in connection with any award or acquisition of shares under a SIP. The participant will have two options:

- Sign the section 431(1) election within 14 days of acquisition so that any benefit received by the participant that represents the difference between the AMV and the UMV is charged to income tax and is payable on acquisition of the restricted securities. In which case any gain on disposal is subject to CGT only; or

- Not sign the election but then any disposal proceeds are multiplied by a percentage that represents the difference between the AMV and the UMV on acquisition and that amount is subject to income tax and possibly NICs on disposal of the shares.

When restricted shares are awarded to, or acquired by the participant under a SIP, the participant does not need to consider the two options above, as the legislation provides a deeming provision in connection with the section 431(1) election. So effectively, the participant is deemed to have signed the election and, as a consequence, any gain on disposal of the restricted shares will only be subject to CGT.

However, the legislation also provides that the deeming provision falls away if income tax is due in certain circumstances. The obvious solution is, therefore, for the participant to sign the election, in any event, even if the company and the participant are not aware of any issues that may give rise to an income tax liability in connection with the SIP.

Employers usually insist that employees sign the section 431(1) election on exercise. Whilst the deeming provision is helpful and even useful when no income tax is due on the exercise, often, both companies and employees choose not to rely on that deeming provision.

*On disposal of the shares?*

Any growth in value of the SIP shares whilst they remain in the SIP trust is not subject to CGT. It therefore follows that if the SIP shares are sold by the SIP trustees whilst in the SIP trust, the participant will be entitled to receive the sale proceeds free from income tax and CGT.

CGT becomes relevant only when the SIP shares are withdrawn from the SIP trust and in respect of any growth in value from that date.

When the shares are ultimately sold or otherwise disposed of by the participant after a period of ownership, CGT may be payable on any gain realised by the participant. CGT is due if the sale proceeds exceed the price that the participant paid on acquisition. The price paid by the participant is the participant's base cost in the shares. However, any amount on which income tax is paid by the participant is added to the base cost of the shares.

*Will the employee qualify for ER?*

The employee may qualify for ER in respect of the gain provided that the employee can demonstrate compliance with the relevant statutory conditions for the relief in terms of employment and holding of shares in the company for at least two years ending with the date of disposal of the shares. As the SIP trustees hold the legal title of the SIP shares on behalf of the employee whilst the employee has the beneficial entitlement to the SIP shares, the employee is treated as if the he or she owns the shares from the award or acquisition date.

In addition, the employee will need to comply with the requirement for the holding of at least 5% of the share capital of the company. It is very highly unlikely that employees receive 5% or more of the ordinary share capital of the company under the SIP so will most probably not be entitled to ER.

# CHAPTER TEN
# UNAPPROVED SCHEMES

## Bonus Scheme/Phantom Option Scheme

Any form of award offered to employees and directors of the company stems from the same overriding wish on the part of both the company and employees. The company wants to incentivise its employees so that overall performance is improved and in return employees expect to be rewarded appropriately for their efforts and contribution to the future success of the company.

In addition to the various approved or tax advantaged schemes discussed above, the company may wish to consider different forms of unapproved or non-tax advantaged schemes. It may do so because the company has already awarded employees and directors with approved or tax advantaged schemes and wishes to reward its employees and directors further. It may also be unable to offer approved schemes because it does not comply with some of the statutory requirement or for any other reason.

Whilst the concept of employee share ownership may be acceptable to some, other shareholders, especially in smaller family businesses may wish to keep ownership in the family. They may wish to pass the company to their children and may not consider a sale of the company at which time employees normally expect to realise value from their shares in the company. In such circumstances, share ownership is not suitable for employees whether approved or otherwise.

The company and its shareholders may still consider the concept of employee incentivisation important for the future success of the company so, whilst not tax efficient, additional cash payments on top of basic salary may be the right option for such companies and their employees.

## Bonus schemes

One of the simplest and easiest to operate fully taxable schemes is a bonus scheme, whether contractual or discretionary. Contractual bonuses provide employees and directors with the certainty of their participation in the scheme and the terms of the scheme whilst discretionary schemes may not offer that certainty. The discretion element of a bonus scheme allows companies to control the circumstances in which employees can receive cash payments from the company.

Either way, bonus schemes are normally awarded to employees and directors of the company subject to the satisfaction of certain performance conditions or objectives. Performance conditions or objectives can be based on performance by employees, the company or both.

## Phantom Option Scheme

A phantom option scheme is a form of bonus scheme whereby employees receive a cash payment which is calculated by reference to the exercise of a share scheme. upon exercise of the phantom option scheme, employees do not receive shares in the company. Instead, they receive a cash payment to which they would have been entitled had they exercised a real share scheme and then sold the newly acquired shares.

A phantom option scheme is, therefore, a form of bonus scheme but is used in order to calculate the cash payment on the date of exercise that relates to the growth in value of the shares above the notional exercise price. For example, employees may be granted phantom options to acquire a number of shares at an agreed exercise price. The exercise price is £10 per share. When the options are exercised, say, three years later, when the value of the shares is £20 per share, employees exercising their phantom options will receive a cash payment of £10 per share.

The phantom option scheme can be drafted and customised for the needs of the company as it wishes. As it is fully taxable, it is not subject to any statutory requirements. It can include any provisions requiring employees to comply with performance conditions before they can exercise their options.

Phantom options can be exercised at any time. Typically, on an exit or at times when the company achieves certain financial goals. The satisfaction of the exercise of phantom options by employees is the responsibility of the company and it is not normally dependent on any other person acquiring the shares in the company. In other words, the company is responsible for the cash payment to employees on exercise of their options. The company will, therefore, need to ensure that it has sufficient cash reserves to satisfy those cash payments.

*Why use a Phantom Option Scheme?*

A company may wish to incentivise employees. However, it may not be comfortable with the concept of employees holding shares in the company. Rather than deal with the complexities of having to establish a new class of shares with restrictions on employees' ability to vote or to receive dividends or establish and operate a more tax efficient share option scheme, A phantom options scheme may be a good alternative.

The exercise price can be determined by reference to any formula that the company may wish to adopt in order to ensure that any value passing to employees on the exercise of their options reflects a real growth in the company's business. The exercise price is not limited to the market value of the shares so the company does not need to concern itself with any valuation issues that may arise when the company establishes an option scheme that results in employees acquiring real shares in the company.

As far as employees are concerned, on exercise of phantom options, employees receive a cash payment from the company whereas on exercise of a real share option scheme, employees are required to fund the exercise price which, may be a challenge for them. They may prefer the certainty of a cash payment from which they can settle any tax liabilities and without the need to concern themselves with share values and other risks associated with the ownership of shares in the company.

*Does the scheme need to be notified?*

Phantom option schemes are not regarded by HMRC as securities or security options for the purposes of the employment related securities regime, as phantom options do not entitle employees to acquire shares in the company on the exercise of their options. Therefore, phantom option schemes do not need to be registered with HMRC. Notification of the scheme is unnecessary until payments are made to employees.

*What are the tax implications?*

The grant of a bonus scheme or phantom options scheme does not give rise to any tax implications for either the employee or the company.

Bonuses and the exercise of phantom options are satisfied by way of cash payments to employees and directors of the company. The payments are normally made by the company and form part of the employee's employment income. The cash payments received by employees are, therefore, subject to the operation of the PAYE system by the employer company which includes the deduction of income tax and both employees' and employer's NICs.

The employer company may be entitled to a corporation tax deduction under general principles in respect of any cash payment to employees and directors of the company.

## Share Option Scheme

The discretionary nature of the non-tax advantaged share option schemes means that companies may grant employees either additional unapproved share option schemes in circumstances where the company has exhausted the grant of approved share option schemes to its employees or where the company does not comply with the relevant statutory requirements for the grant of approved share option schemes.

The grant of non-tax advantaged share option schemes allows companies to award their employees with options to acquire shares in the company without the need to consider any of the statutory requirements that are relevant to tax advantaged share option schemes. Obviously, any transaction in shares will be subject to any relevant company law or other regulatory requirements.

Given that such share option schemes are, in principle, fully taxable, they are normally exercisable on the sale of the shares of the company or at a time when the company is listed on the stock market. At that time, employees are able to realise value from the disposal of their shares which, may allow them to satisfy any tax liabilities that may arise on the exercise of their options.

Such schemes may also be exercised at any time, normally at the discretion of the company, and structured in such a way as to ensure that employees suffer no or very little liability to tax on exercise of the options or acquisition of shares in the company.

A non-tax advantaged share option scheme may include any of the features of the approved option schemes. Companies can set any performance conditions before options can be exercised by employees and it can limit the number of shares or the identity of the employees who may be able to participate in the scheme.

A share option scheme can therefore be very similar and even based on a CSOP save that employees or participants in the scheme receive no tax benefits other than the ability to acquire shares in the company in the future. Indeed, an invalid EMI scheme or any EMI options granted over the relevant individual limit will be regarded as unapproved with the same consequences as for any unapproved or non-tax advantaged share option scheme.

*Do the shares need to be valued?*

Shares in the company need to be valued for the purpose of any share option scheme or otherwise in respect of any transaction in shares. Valuation of the shares is not a statutory requirement but is highly recommended in any event.

An unapproved share option scheme is taxable. For this reason valuation is crucial as valuation of the shares will be needed when the options are exercised.

Valuation of the shares helps determine the exercise price and is necessary to determine the income tax liability of the employee if the options or any part of them become subject to income tax either on any benefit received by employees or by reference to the restricted securities regime.

As the non-tax advantaged share option scheme is not subject to any statutory requirements, the exercise price does not have to be set by reference to the market value of the shares on the date of grant of the options. Income tax will be payable by employees on any benefit received by them on exercise of the options. The benefit is calculated by reference to the difference between the exercise price and the market value of the shares on the date of exercise.

Companies, therefore, need to obtain, preferably, independent valuation of the shares in the company both the AMV and the UMV when unapproved options are granted to employees of the company. Given the unapproved nature of the scheme, the company is not able to agree valuation with HMRC before unapproved options are granted to employees so the company will need to ensure that any such valuation is properly undertaken.

As for listed companies, the market value can easily be determined by reference to the published value of the shares at the relevant date.

*Does the scheme need to be notified?*

Following the grant of non-taxed advantaged share options to employees, the company must notify HMRC. The notification must be done online through the ERS online filing system and, in respect of the first registration and notification, the company must make the notification by the 6 July following the end of the tax year in which a reportable event occurs during that tax year. The scheme can still be registered and notified to HMRC by the 6 July following the end of the tax year in which it is implemented.

The company must register all non-tax advantaged share option schemes with HMRC. It may do so separately in respect of each non-tax advantaged scheme or register all of them under the same registration number. If all non-tax advantaged share schemes are registered under the same registration number, the company will need to file one annual return. Otherwise, the company will need to file an annual return in respect of each of the non-tax advantaged schemes.

The company is also required to complete online annual returns. All annual returns must be submitted by 6 July after the end of the relevant tax year. The company must notify any changes to the scheme including exercise of options, release or lapse of options, any exchange of options or any other adjustment to any of the options.

The company must complete the annual return even if there have been no changes that require notification.

Tax Implications

*For the Company –*

The company will, normally, be entitled to a statutory corporation tax deduction in connection with the non-tax advantaged share option scheme. The company can deduct an amount equal to the benefit obtained by the employee when the options are exercised. This is the most valuable deduction the company can get in connection with the scheme. However, if the company wishes to get a deduction for the amounts spent on setting up the scheme and the operation of the scheme throughout its life, the company may need to rely on general principles of corporation tax deduction.

In a group structure, the employee may exercise options to acquire shares in a company which is not the employer of that employee. The corporation tax deduction can only be claimed by the employer company and not by the company in which the employee acquires shares.

The corporation tax deduction can only be claimed in the accounting period in which shares are allotted or transferred to the employee, which, normally, occurs in the accounting period when the exercise of the options takes place.

*For the employee –*

Given that the scheme is a non-tax advantaged one, the employee is not entitled to any tax reliefs on any benefits received under the scheme. Therefore, the following expected tax implications will arise on exercise of options under the unapproved share option scheme.

*On the date of grant?*

There are no tax implications when options are granted to employees.

*On exercise?*

When options are exercised by the employee, income tax will be payable on the difference between the AMV of the shares acquired and the exercise price actually paid by the employee.

*NICs liability?*

If at the time of exercise of the options, the shares are RCAs, the employee's employer will be required to operate the PAYE system and deduct the income tax due from the employee together with the relevant amount representing Class 1 employee's NICs and also account to HMRC for Class 1 employer's NICs.

The shares of listed companies or companies listed on AIM are always RCAs. For this reason, the NICs liability of the employer and the obligation to operate the PAYE system will always apply to those shares.

If an income tax liability arises in connection with the exercise of the shares in circumstances where the employer company is required to operate the PAYE system and deduct the amount of income tax from the employee together with primary Class 1 NICs, the employer will need to pay to HMRC the amount deducted together with the secondary Class 1 NICs. However, the employer may recover its liability in respect of the secondary Class 1 NICs from the employee. It can do so either by way of recovery from the employee or by transferring it to the employee.

If an income tax liability arises, in connection with the acquisition of shares following exercise of the option, in circumstances where the employer company is not required to operate the PAYE system, the employee will need to complete a self-assessment tax return and pay income tax. No NICs are payable in such circumstances.

*What if the shares are restricted securities?*

Shares acquired by employees following an exercise of options awarded under an unapproved share option scheme are very likely to be restricted securities and therefore subject to the restricted securities regime.

In order to avoid the charge under the restricted securities regime, the employee needs to consider signing the section 431(1) election.

The employee acquiring restricted securities following an exercise of options under an unapproved share option scheme may wish to consider the implications of the restricted securities regime. The employee will have two options:

- Sign the section 431(1) election within 14 days of acquisition so that any benefit received by the employee that represents the difference between the AMV and the UMV is charged to income tax and is payable on acquisition of the restricted securities. In which case any gain on disposal is subject to CGT only; or

- Not sign the election but then any disposal proceeds are multiplied by a percentage that represents the difference between the AMV and the UMV on acquisition and that amount is subject to income tax and possibly NICs on disposal of the shares.

There is no equivalent deeming provision in respect of the acquisition of restricted securities following exercise of options under an unapproved share option scheme, as is the case with approved option schemes. Therefore, the employee will need to consider signing the election in any event. The company may require employees to sign the section 431(1) election on exercise.

*On disposal of the shares?*

When the shares are ultimately sold or otherwise disposed of by the employee (now shareholder), either immediately following exercise of the options or after a period of ownership, CGT may be payable on any gain realised by that shareholder.

CGT is due if the sale proceeds exceed the price that the employee paid on exercise of the options. The price paid by the employee on exercise is the employee's base cost in the shares. However, any amount on which income tax is paid by the employee together with any liability of the employer to Class 1 NICs that is transferred to the employee is added to the base cost of the shares.

If shares, acquired under an unapproved share option scheme, are disposed of by the employee immediately after acquisition, CGT is not likely to arise, as the liability of the employee to income tax on any benefit will result in the base cost in the shares being equal to the market value of the shares on disposal.

*Will the employee qualify for ER?*

The employee may qualify for ER in respect of the gain provided that the employee can demonstrate compliance with the relevant statutory conditions for the relief in terms of employment and holding of shares in the company for at least two years ending with the date of disposal of the shares.

In addition, and, unlike EMI, the requirement for the holding of at least 5% of the share capital is still relevant to employees acquiring shares in the company under the unapproved share option scheme. Therefore, if an employee under the unapproved share option scheme receives options to acquire shares that represent less than 5% of the ordinary share capital of the company, the employee will not be entitled to claim the ER.

## Joint Ownership Arrangement (JOA)

A JOA is an incentive arrangement under which employees acquire shares in a company jointly with another person, typically, an EBT. The acquisition is not subject to an option and shares are transferred to the co-owners from the outset. Under the arrangement, employees acquire an interest in the shares. That interest entitles them to participate in the growth in value of the shares only. The effect of the arrangement, therefore, is to limit any tax liability of the participating employees to CGT only. If the arrangement is implemented correctly, employees' gain will not be subject to income tax.

The co-owner of the shares under a JOA can be any individual or company. An EBT is normally used as the co-owner in order to ensure that shares can be transferred to the EBT in circumstances where the employee is required to dispose of the shares when, for example, the employee ceases to be employed by the company. The shares can then be held by the EBT for other beneficiaries of the EBT either in respect of the JOA or any other scheme. Other co-owners such as an individual or a company may end up holding the shares but their ownership will serve no purpose to the company, more particularly, for the purposes of the JOA.

A JOA is normally made with senior employees of the company in order to incentivise them either further in circumstances where they've already exhausted their entitlement to acquire shares under any of the approved options or where such approved arrangements are not available.

The JOA is based on the growth in value of the jointly owned shares from the date of acquisition of the shares. It is therefore important that companies and senior employees consider the likelihood of the shares going up in value before they implement and operate such arrangements.

The JOA is also based on any gain on disposal of the shares by the senior employee being subject to CGT rather than income tax. If income tax is payable on acquisition by the senior employee, that income tax liability needs to be sufficiently small to make the arrangement viable as far as the senior employee is concerned.

The employee and the EBT will enter into a joint ownership agreement. The joint ownership agreement can be drafted and customised in any way as to the arrangement with the senior employee and will set out the specific arrangements between the EBT and the senior employee in respect of the jointly owned shares. In its basic form, the agreement will include provisions which:

- Define the interest split between the co-owners and how the proceeds of sale are divided between them when the shares are sold;

- Confirm the arrangement whereby the senior employee is entitled to participate in the growth in value of the shares above an agreed level. The agreed level will normally be the current market value of the shares on the date of acquisition of the shares.

The JOA may include additional provisions restricting the ability of the senior employee from realising value until the expiry of a certain period of time or by reference to performance conditions. Whilst the senior employee owns an interest in the shares from the outset, the co-owner, the EBT, may be entitled to acquire a certain proportion of the senior employee's interest in the shares or the whole of the interest if certain conditions are not met.

The company may or may not add any such provisions but if it does it may normally deal with any such provisions in a separate agreement with the senior employee even though such provisions can form part of the joint ownership agreement.

JOAs are more popular with public companies. Public companies are more restricted in their ability to create complicated classes of shares so may not be able to operate growth shares arrangements as referred to in the next chapter but they may achieve similar results by using a JOA.

*Do the shares need to be valued?*

Shares in the company need to be valued for the purpose of any share option scheme or otherwise in respect of any transaction in shares. Valuation of the shares is not a statutory requirement but is highly recommended in any event. Valuation of the shares helps determine the income tax liability of the employee if the acquisition of the jointly owned shares or any part of it becomes subject to income tax either on any benefit received by employees or by reference to the restricted securities regime.

As the JOA is a form of non-tax advantaged arrangement, it is not subject to any statutory requirements, the value of the interest acquired by the senior employee does not have to be set by reference to the market value of that interest on the date it is acquired by the employee. However, the arrangement is based on the employee acquiring that interest at its market value so that no income tax is payable on acquisition.

Income tax will be payable by employees on any benefit received by them on acquisition. The benefit is calculated by reference to the difference between the acquisition price paid by the employee and the AMV of the shares on the acquisition date.

Companies, therefore, need to obtain independent valuation of the shares in the company both the AMV and the UMV when any transaction in shares occurs more specifically between the company and its employees.

Given the unapproved nature of the arrangement, the company is not able to agree valuation with HMRC before unapproved arrangements take place so the company will need to ensure that any such valuation is properly undertaken.

It is crucial for the viability of the JOA particularly because the senior employee acquires an interest in shares that entitles him or her to receive the growth in value of the shares. To avoid any liability to income tax or to keep any such liability to a minimum, the value of the interest will need to be as accurate as possible. For this reason, the company needs to consider using the services of a specialist share valuer who is experienced in valuing shares that are used in arrangements that rely on future growth value.

Whilst listed companies can easily access the market value of their ordinary shares, the interest acquired will still need to be valued.

*Does the JOA need to be notified?*

The company must notify HMRC when it issues employment related securities to its employees. The notification must be done online through the ERS online filing system and, in respect of the first registration and notification, the company must make the notification by the 6 July following the end of the tax year in which a reportable event occurs during that tax year. The scheme can still be registered and notified to HMRC by the 6 July following the end of the tax year in which it is implemented.

The company must register all non-tax advantaged share option schemes with HMRC. It may do so separately in respect of each non-tax advantaged scheme or register all of them under the same registration number. If all non-tax advantaged share schemes are registered under the same registration number, the company will need to file one annual return. Otherwise, the company will need to file an annual return in respect of each of the non-tax advantaged schemes.

The company is also required to complete online annual returns. All annual returns must be submitted by 6 July after the end of the relevant tax year. The company must notify any changes that may affect the holding of shares in the company.

The company must complete the annual return even if there have been no changes that require notification.

Tax Implications

*For the Company –*

The company will not be entitled to a corporation tax deduction in connection with the JOA if the arrangement results in the senior employee's gain being subject to CGT only.

The company can deduct an amount equal to the benefit obtained by the employee but only in circumstances where income tax is payable by the employee on that benefit. This is the most valuable deduction the company can get in connection with the arrangement. However, the company will be able to obtain a deduction in respect of much smaller amounts on which the employee may be required to pay income tax.

In a group structure, the employee may acquire shares in a company which is not the employer of that employee. The corporation tax deduction can only be claimed by the employer company and not by the company in which the employee acquires shares.

The corporation tax deduction can only be claimed in the accounting period in which shares (or interest in shares) are allotted or transferred to the employee, which, normally, occurs in the accounting period in which shares are acquired and income tax is paid by employees.

*For the employee –*

The JOA is a very tax efficient arrangement, as it is undertaken on the basis that any liability of the senior employee is limited to CGT (and perhaps, relatively, small amount of income tax) rather than income tax. Given that the arrangement is a non-tax advantaged one in terms of any statutory tax reliefs, the employee is not entitled to any tax reliefs on any benefits received under the JOA. Therefore, the following expected tax implications will arise on the acquisition of an interest in the jointly owned shares under the JOA.

*Income tax liability?*

The senior employee will suffer an income tax liability if the interest in the jointly owned shares is acquired for less than the market value of the shares. Any income tax liability is calculated by reference to the difference between the price paid by the senior employee and the market value of the interest in the shares on acquisition.

*NICs liability?*

If income tax is due on the acquisition of the interest in the jointly owned shares and, at the time of acquisition, the shares are RCAs, the employee's employer will be required to operate the PAYE system and deduct the income tax due from the employee together with the relevant amount representing Class 1 employee's NICs and also account to HMRC for Class 1 employer's NICs.

The shares of listed companies or companies listed on AIM are always RCAs. For this reason, the NICs liability of the employer and the obligation to operate the PAYE system will always apply to those shares.

If an income tax liability arises in connection with the acquisition in circumstances where the employer company is not required to operate the PAYE system, the employee will need to complete a self-assessment tax return and pay income tax. No NICs are payable in such circumstances.

*What if the shares are restricted securities?*

An interest in the jointly owned shares acquired by employees under a JOA are likely to be restricted securities as they will very likely be subject to a risk of forfeiture and therefore subject to the restricted securities regime.

In order to avoid the charge under the restricted securities regime and ensure that any growth in value of the shares is subject to CGT only, the employee needs to opt out of the regime even if the employee agrees to pay the full UMV of the interest in the jointly owned shares.

The employee will, therefore, need to sign the section 431(1) election, within 14 days of acquisition of the interest and pay the income tax on the difference between the AMV and the UMV of the interest in the shares, if any, so that any benefit received by the employee that represents the difference between the AMV and the UMV is charged to income tax on acquisition of the restricted securities thereby ensuring that any gain on disposal is subject to CGT only.

Otherwise, in circumstances where the employee has not paid the full UMV of the interest in the shares or if HMRC concludes that any amount paid does not reflect the true UMV of the interest in the shares and the employee has not signed the section 431(1) election within the requisite 14 days period, any disposal proceeds received by the senior employee will be multiplied by a percentage that represents the difference between the AMV and the UMV on acquisition of the interest and that amount is subject to income tax and, possibly, NICs on disposal of the interest in the shares.

*On disposal of the shares?*

When the interest in the jointly owned shares is ultimately sold or otherwise disposed of by the employee after a period of ownership, CGT may be payable on any gain realised by that employee.

CGT is due if the sale proceeds exceed the price that the employee paid on acquisition of the interest in the shares. The price paid by the employee on acquisition is the employee's base cost in the interest in the shares. However, any amount on which income tax is paid by the employee, whether in respect of any discount to the AMV of the interest in the shares or in respect of the opting out of the restricted securities regime, is added to the base cost of the shares.

*Will the employee qualify for ER?*

ER applies to the disposal of an interest in shares in the company so the employee may qualify for ER in respect of the gain provided that the employee can demonstrate compliance with the relevant statutory conditions for the relief in terms of employment and holding of the interest in the jointly owned shares in the company for at least two years ending with the date of disposal of the interest in the shares. In addition, the employee is required to satisfy the requirement for the holding of at least 5% of the share capital in the company.

As the shares are held jointly with the trustees of the EBT, the employee's percentage holding is limited to the interest that the employee has in the shares. This is likely to be much less than 5% of the issued share capital of the company. This is because the starting point of the employee's holding is zero or nearly zero as the interest that the employee has in the shares grows over time as the value of the shares exceeds the value on acquisition. For this reason, the employee will most probably not be entitled to claim the ER in respect of the gain on disposal of the interest in the jointly owned shares.

## Growth Shares

The concept of growth shares is very similar to a JOA in terms of the employee's expectation to hold shares in the company with a very low initial value benefiting from the rise in value of the shares from the date of issue ensuring that any future gain is only subject to CGT. However, the structure of growth shares is a very different from a JOA.

Under a JOA, the employee acquirers an interest in ordinary shares that are jointly held with an EBT. Growth shares, on the other hand, are ordinary shares of a special class which entitle the holders of growth shares to benefit from the growth in the value of the company from the date of issue of the shares.

To put it simply, the market value of the company is determined at the time growth shares are issued to employees or senior employees of the company. On a future sale or on a winding up of the company, the holders of growth shares will be entitled to share in the value of the company above that market value.

For example, a company with a market value of £1 million issues growth shares to five of its senior employees. The company is later sold for £3 million. The £3 million proceeds will be divided as to £1 million to any current shareholders of the company not including the holders of growth shares with the remaining £2 million divided amongst all the shareholders including the holders of growth shares.

Growth shares are normally offered to senior employees of the company at a time when the company is quite valuable and senior employees may not be able to afford to acquire shares at their market value. Other approved options may have been exhausted or not available and other unapproved options may have been discounted by the company or its senior employees whether on the basis that the option route may not be the best way forward given the income tax implications that may arise on the exercise of the options or due to the perceived complexity of any of the other arrangements.

Growth shares are very popular with private companies, as they can create more than one class of shares. Public companies are more restricted in their ability to create complicated classes of shares but they may achieve similar results by using a JOA.

The acquisition of growth shares by such individuals may be ideal as it provides a tax efficient way for them to acquire shares in the company with a very low value which may or may not be subject to income tax. If implemented correctly, any future value will only be subject to CGT.

The issue of growth shares by the company may also be ideal for existing shareholders. Whilst incentivising senior employees, existing shareholders are protected from dilution by ring fencing their current value in the company. Any future value is then shared with the holders of growth shares.

The issue by the company of growth shares is based on the growth in value of the company from the date of acquisition of the growth shares. It is therefore important that companies and senior employees consider the likelihood of the value the company going up before they implement and operate such arrangement.

Additionally, the issue of growth shares is based on any gain on disposal of the shares by the senior employee being subject to CGT rather than income tax. If income tax is payable on acquisition by the senior employee, that income tax liability needs to be sufficiently small to make the arrangement viable as far as the senior employee is concerned.

In order to achieve the desired results, the company will need to amend its articles of association, create a new class of growth shares and include provisions setting out the rights and obligations that are attached to the growth shares. The company will need to consider the following provisions:

- The ability of the holders of growth shares to receive dividends or be able to vote. The ability to receive dividends or to vote, if allowed, will need to be carefully calculated by reference to the proportion of the value which the growth shares represent to the overall value of the company;

- The company may also wish to add good or bad leaver provisions to its articles of association in order to clarify the position in circumstances where the senior employee ceases to be employed by the company. Such provisions may require the senior employee to offer the growth shares for sale at the lower of market value at the time of sale or the original acquisition cost. The method of calculation will depend on the reason for leaving.

Other than company law issues and, perhaps, regulatory provisions, there are no statutory requirements that are applicable to growth shares. They are quite flexible and can be designed to suit the company's requirements as to its arrangements with its senior employees. They can be offered to a select few including consultants and non-executive directors and on different terms. However, the scheme will not be an employee's share scheme and may not get the benefit of the various company law and financial services exemptions.

They can be issued subject to performance conditions and other time-based restrictions so that additional rights can be received by holders of growth shares in terms of rights to dividends and voting when such conditions and restrictions are achieved.

*Do the shares need to be valued?*

Ordinarily, any transaction involving shares in the company, that may give rise to a tax liability, should be valued in any event. Valuation of the shares is not a statutory requirement but is highly recommended. Valuation of the shares helps determine the income tax liability of the employee if the acquisition of the growth shares or any part of it becomes subject to income tax either on any benefit received by employees or by reference to the restricted securities regime.

As the issue of growth shares in the company is a form of non-tax advantaged arrangement, it is not subject to any statutory requirements. The value of the shares acquired by the employee does not have to be set by reference to the market value of the shares on the date they are acquired by the employee.

Income tax will be payable on any benefit received by the employee on acquisition. The benefit is calculated by reference to the difference between the acquisition price paid by the employee and the UMV of the shares on the acquisition date. In order to avoid any liability to income tax, the employee will need to pay the UMV of the shares on acquisition.

The growth shares arrangement is based on the employee paying no income tax or very little income tax on the acquisition of the growth shares. For this reason, companies need to obtain independent valuation of the shares in the company both the AMV and the UMV when any transaction in shares occurs more specifically between the company and its employees.

Given the unapproved nature of the arrangement, the company is not able to agree valuation with HMRC before unapproved arrangements take place so the company will need to ensure that any such valuation is properly undertaken. It is crucial for the viability of the growth shares arrangement particularly because the employee acquires shares that entitle him or her to participate in the future growth in value of the company.

To avoid any liability to income tax or to keep any such liability to a minimum, the value of the shares will need to be as accurate as possible. The company needs to consider using the services of a specialist share valuer who is experienced in valuing shares that are used in such arrangements that rely on future growth value.

The immediate assumption, when the value of the growth shares is considered, is that the value must be nil because, on day one, the holder of growth shares has nothing. No value from which the holder can receive any benefit. However, the growth shares may have a 'hope' value. This is a tangible value that must be taken into account when growth shares are valued. Growth shares in a company that is fast growing will, quite possibly, be more valuable than growth shares in a company that has no real prospect of growth in the foreseeable future.

Let's look at the following example that may illustrate the 'hope' value point. A well-known Hollywood actor decides to donate all of his or her money to charity. The actor's bank account is now empty. The actor is now looking for a new role in a film. The actor, who is normally very busy, is very likely to find a very highly paid job relatively quickly. On the other hand, a new actor may struggle to find a job and, in any event, may not be well paid. The well-known actor has that 'hope' value whereas the new actor may not have it to quite the same extent.

Valuation of growth shares may not be a simple exercise. However, some companies issue employees with hurdle shares in order to ensure that the value of the shares is even lower. Hurdle shares are similar to growth shares. The main difference between them is that the holder of hurdle shares can participate in the growth in value of the company when the value of the company exceeds an amount that is higher than the company's current value.

For example, if the company's current value is £1 million. Growth shares will normally entitle the holder to participate in any future growth over £1 million. Hurdle shares will entitle the holder to participate in any future growth over, say, £1.2 million.

*Does the growth shares arrangement need to be notified?*

The company must notify HMRC when it issues employment related securities to its employees. The notification must be done online through the ERS online filing system and, in respect of the first registration and notification, the company must make the notification by the 6 July following the end of the tax year in which a reportable event occurs during that tax year. The scheme can still be registered and notified to HMRC by the 6 July following the end of the tax year in which it is implemented.

The company must register all non-tax advantaged share option schemes with HMRC. It may do so separately in respect of each non-tax advantaged scheme or register all of them under the same registration number. If all non-tax advantaged share schemes are registered under the same registration number, the company will need to file one annual return. Otherwise, the company will need to file an annual return in respect of each of the non-tax advantaged schemes.

The company is also required to complete online annual returns. All annual returns must be submitted by 6 July after the end of the relevant tax year. The company must notify any changes that may affect the holding of shares in the company.

The company must complete the annual return even if there have been no changes that require notification.

## Tax Implications

*For the Company –*

The company will not be entitled to a corporation tax deduction in connection with the growth shares if the arrangement results in the employee's gain being subject to CGT only. The company can deduct an amount equal to the benefit obtained by the employee but only in circumstances where income tax is payable by the employee on that benefit. This is the most valuable deduction the company can get in connection with the arrangement. However, the company will be able to obtain a deduction in respect of much smaller amounts on which the employee may be required to pay income tax.

In a group structure, the employee may acquire shares in a company which is not the employer of that employee. The corporation tax deduction can only be claimed by the employer company and not by the company in which the employee acquires shares.

The corporation tax deduction can only be claimed in the accounting period in which shares are allotted to the employee, which, normally, occurs in the accounting period in which shares are acquired and income tax is paid by employees.

*For the employee –*

Like the JOA, the issue of growth shares by a company is more tax efficient than other non-tax efficient option arrangements. It is based on the employee acquiring shares with no, or very little value with any liability being limited to CGT (and perhaps, relatively, small amount of income tax) rather than income tax.

Given that the arrangement is a non-tax advantaged one in terms of any statutory tax reliefs, the employee is not entitled to any tax reliefs on any benefits received under the growth shares arrangement. Therefore, the following expected tax implications will arise on the acquisition of growth shares in the company.

*Income tax liability?*

The employee will suffer an income tax liability if the growth shares are acquired for less than the market value of the shares. Any income tax liability is calculated by reference to the difference between the price paid by the employee and the market value of the shares on acquisition.

*NICs liability?*

If income tax is due on the acquisition of the growth shares and, at the time of acquisition, the shares are RCAs, the employee's employer will be required to operate the PAYE system and deduct the income tax due from the employee together with the relevant amount representing Class 1 employee's NICs and also account to HMRC for Class 1 employer's NICs. Any income tax is calculated by reference to the best reasonable estimate of the tax liability.

If an income tax liability arises in connection with the acquisition in circumstances where the employer company is not required to operate the PAYE system, the employee will need to complete a self-assessment tax return and pay income tax. No NICs are payable in such circumstances.

*What if the shares are restricted securities?*

Growth shares acquired by employees are likely to be restricted securities as they will very likely be subject to a risk of forfeiture and therefore subject to the restricted securities regime.

In order to avoid the charge under the restricted securities regime and ensure that any growth in value of the shares is subject to CGT only, the employee needs to opt out of the regime even if the employee agrees to pay the full UMV of the growth shares. The employee will, therefore, need to sign the section 431(1) election, within 14 days of acquisition of the growth shares and pay the income tax on the difference between the AMV and the UMV of the growth shares, if any, so that any benefit received by the employee that represents the difference between the AMV and the UMV is charged to income tax on acquisition of the restricted securities thereby ensuring that any gain on disposal is subject to CGT only.

Otherwise, if the employee does not pay the full UMV of the growth shares or if HMRC concludes that any amount paid does not reflect the true UMV of the growth shares and the employee has not signed the section 431(1) election within the requisite 14 days period, any disposal proceeds received by the employee will be multiplied by a percentage that represents the difference between the AMV and the UMV on acquisition of the growth shares and that amount is subject to income tax and possibly NICs on disposal of the growth shares.

*On disposal of the shares?*

When the growth shares are ultimately sold or otherwise disposed of by the employee after a period of ownership, CGT may be payable on any gain realised by that employee. CGT is due if the sale proceeds exceed the price that the employee paid on acquisition of the growth shares.

The price paid by the employee on acquisition is the employee's base cost in the growth shares. However, any amount on which income tax is paid by the employee, whether in respect of any discount to the AMV of the growth shares or in respect of the opting out of the restricted securities regime, is added to the base cost of the shares.

*Will the employee qualify for ER?*

ER applies to the disposal of shares in the company so the employee may qualify for ER in respect of the gain provided that the employee can demonstrate compliance with the relevant statutory conditions for the relief in terms of employment and holding of the growth shares in the company for at least two years ending with the date of disposal of the growth shares. In addition, the employee is required to satisfy the requirement for the holding of at least 5% of the ordinary share capital in the company.

Some companies used to give holders of growth shares enhanced voting rights in order to enable them to get the required 5% shareholding in the company and so have the benefit of ER.

With effect from 29 October 2018, two additional economic tests have been added beyond the requirement for 5% in terms of voting rights. For this reason, employees who hold growth shares in the company that represent less than 5% of the issued share capital of the company will most probably not be entitled to claim the ER in respect of the gain on disposal of the growth shares.

*Growth shares and EMI?*

EMI options can be granted over growth shares. This is particularly useful for three main reasons:

- The market value of growth shares compared with the other ordinary share capital of the company is very likely to be very low. This means that the company can grant more EMI options within the qualifying employees' individual limit;

- Holders of growth shares are more likely to successfully claim ER on disposal of the growth shares under the EMI umbrella as they do not need to be concerned with the 5% shareholding requirement;

- The valuation of the growth shares is complex and could potentially be challenged at a time when growth shares have already been issued. The value of growth shares cannot be agreed with HMRC in advance so companies may have to issue growth shares and rely on the valuation that they obtain for that purpose. This may be risky. However, if growth shares are used in an EMI scheme, the market value of the growth shares, both the AMV and the UMV can be agreed with HMRC in advance.

## Nil Paid Shares

A private company can issue shares to its employees or senior employees without the latter having to pay the nominal value or any premium on the shares, i.e. nil paid or partly paid. In other words, shares are normally issued by a company fully paid but the company may agree that the price of the shares, or part of it, can be paid in the future when the company makes a call for that payment to be made.

A public company is not allowed to legally issue nil paid shares but may be able to issue partly paid shares provided that the minimum payment requirement is strictly observed by the company and its employees. However, a public company may be able to issue nil paid shares if the arrangement is structured as an employees' share scheme. This means that a public company may only issue nil paid shares to its employees or former employees but not to consultants or non-executive directors.

Other regulatory and listing rules may prevent public companies from issuing nil or partly paid shares to its employees so the arrangement is mainly used by private companies.

The issue by a company to its employees or any of them of nil paid shares is meant to resolve one of the main reasons for the company operating any form of share schemes. Employees may struggle with the upfront payment for the shares of an established company. Unless they pay the full UMV, which may prove prohibitive for some, employees may need to find the income tax and, possibly, NICs on the value of any discount to the market value of the shares.

The issue by a company of nil paid shares does not require any upfront payment by employees. The issue of partly paid shares will result in the employees having to pay a small amount upfront with any balance being left outstanding until such time when the company decides to make a call for the payment of the balance.

Nil paid shares are more popular than partly paid shares and are normally offered to senior employees of the company at a time when the company is quite valuable and senior employees may not be able to afford to acquire shares at their market value.

Other approved options may have been exhausted or not available and other unapproved options may have been discounted by the company or its senior employees whether on the basis that the option route may not be the best way forward given the income tax implications that may arise on the exercise of the options or due to the perceived complexity of any of the other arrangements.

The issue by a company of nil paid shares offer employees an immediate share ownership in the company. If structured correctly so that no income tax arises on acquisition of nil paid shares, any rise in value of nil paid shares from the acquisition date will be subject to CGT only.

*What is the catch?*

Whilst seemingly ideal as far as employees or senior employees of the company are concerned, the nil paid shares arrangement between a company and its employees is not a disguise for the issue of free shares to employees of the company. Under the arrangement, employees agree to pay to the company the full UMV of the shares in order to ensure that there is no liability to income tax on any part of the market value of the shares which may be treated as issued to employees at an under-value.

When the company makes a call on the employees to pay any out-standing balance on the shares, employees will be under a legal obligation to make that payment. This means that, in circumstances where any such call is made by the company at a time when the market value of the shares in the company has gone down, employees will still be under a legal obligation to pay the full UMV of the shares that they agreed to pay on acquisition of the nil paid shares.

In addition to the above, if the company is liquidated, a liquidator of the company is very likely to make a call on the employees for the payment of any outstanding balance on the nil paid shares. Notwithstanding any restrictions on the company in its articles of association in terms of its ability to make a call for the payment of any unpaid amount on the nil or partly paid shares, a liquidator will not be bound by such restrictions.

Therefore, when a liquidator makes a call for any outstanding balance to be paid, employees will need to find the money and pay it to the company within the requisite period of time. Additionally, as the company is in liquidation, employees may end up disposing of their shares for a loss but without any discount being allowed on the full UMV which they agreed to pay on acquisition of the nil or partly paid shares.

This is a risk that employees will need to consider very carefully when acquiring nil paid shares in the company. The expectation of the employees is that any rise in value of the market value of the shares is subject to CGT but such expectation needs to be real and more likely than the company going the other way, slowing down and losing value, or worst still, going down the liquidation route.

Obviously, from the outset, the reason for the issue of shares by the company to its senior employees is in order to incentivise the employees and to encourage them to help drive the business of the company forward so any loss that the senior employees may suffer as a result of the market value of the shares in the company going down or otherwise as a consequence of the company's liquidation may be down to them and their inability to drive the business of the company forward and to a successful future as may have been previously envisaged by the shareholders of the company.

Contrast the nil paid shares arrangement with an option scheme. An option scheme allows employees to have the flexibility of deciding whether or not to exercise their options in the company. When employees are able to exercise their options in the company, they can consider the exercise price by reference to the market value of the company at that time together with other factors as to the viability of exercising their options. If it makes financial sense, they will probably choose to exercise their options. Otherwise, they may wish to delay the exercise to a later date in the future when the shares have gone up in value or simply abandon their options altogether and allow them to lapse.

On the other hand, an unapproved share option scheme will result in the employees having to pay income tax and, possibly, NICs on exercise on the difference between the exercise price and the market value of the shares on the date of exercise. The nil paid shares arrangement is obviously more tax efficient to employees but only in circumstances where no income tax arises on the acquisition and provided that the nil paid shares arrangement is not entered into on the basis that the avoidance or saving of tax or NICs is the main reason or one of the main reasons for the arrangement in which case, an immediate income tax may be due on any benefit received by the employees.

The company will need to amend its articles of association in order to allow and authorise the issue of nil paid shares or partly paid shares to its employees. The company will also need to consider whether or not holders of nil or partly paid shares are entitled to vote or to receive dividends in respect of their holding of nil or partly paid shares in the company.

Provisions for the call on the employees to make a payment of the full UMV on the shares will need to be included in the articles of association in order to ensure that participating employees are contractually obliged to make the payment within the time frames set out by the company's articles of association.

The company will need to consider whether any amount outstanding should be payable by demand when the company decides to call for the payment of the outstanding amount, which can happen at any time or whether to set the repayment date or dates by reference to specific events such as a certain number of years after acquisition of the nil or partly paid shares, on a sale of the company, listing or on cessation of employment.

A failure by employees to pay any outstanding balance on the nil or partly paid shares following a call by the company for the payment of any outstanding balance on the shares may lead to their shares being forfeited.

*Do the shares need to be valued?*

Ordinarily, any transaction involving shares in the company, that may give rise to a tax liability, should be valued in any event. Valuation of the shares is not a statutory requirement but is highly recommended. Valuation of the shares helps determine the income tax liability of the employee if the acquisition of nil or partly paid shares or any part of it becomes subject to income tax either on any benefit received by employees or by reference to the restricted securities regime.

As the issue of nil or partly paid shares in the company is a form of non-tax advantaged arrangement, it is not subject to any statutory requirements. The value of the shares acquired by the employee does not have to be set by reference to the market value of the nil or partly paid shares on the date they are acquired by the employee. However, the arrangement is based on the employee agreeing to pay the full UMV of the shares in order to avoid any income tax charge on acquisition of the shares.

Income tax will be payable on any benefit received by the employee on acquisition if the employee pays less than the full UMV of the shares when the company makes a call for the payment of any outstanding balance on the shares or if the shares are acquired with an avoidance motive.

The benefit is calculated by reference to the difference between the acquisition price paid by the employee and the UMV of the shares on the acquisition date. In order to avoid any liability to income tax, the employee will need to agree to pay the full UMV of the shares on acquisition.

The company will need to obtain independent valuation of the shares in the company both the AMV and the UMV when any transaction in shares occurs more specifically between the company and its employees.

Given the unapproved nature of the arrangement, the company is not able to agree valuation with HMRC before unapproved arrangements take place so the company will need to ensure that any such valuation is properly undertaken. To avoid any liability to income tax or to keep any such liability to a minimum, the value of the shares will need to be as accurate as possible.

As for listed companies, the market value can easily be determined by reference to the published value of the shares at the relevant date.

*Does the nil or partly paid shares arrangement need to be notified?*

The company must notify HMRC when it issues employment related securities to its employees. The notification must be done online through the ERS online filing system and, in respect of the first registration and notification, the company must make the notification by the 6 July following the end of the tax year in which a reportable event occurs during that tax year. The scheme can still be registered and notified to HMRC by the 6 July following the end of the tax year in which it is implemented.

The company must register all non-tax advantaged share option schemes with HMRC. It may do so separately in respect of each non-tax advantaged scheme or register all of them under the same registration number. If all non-tax advantaged share schemes are registered under the same registration number, the company will need to file one annual return. Otherwise, the company will need to file an annual return in respect of each of the non-tax advantaged schemes.

The company is also required to complete online annual returns. All annual returns must be submitted by 6 July after the end of the relevant tax year. The company must notify any changes that may affect the holding of shares in the company.

The company must complete the annual return even if there have been no changes that require notification.

## Tax Implications

*For the Company –*

The company will not be entitled to a corporation tax deduction in connection with the nil or partly paid shares arrangement. This is due to the fact that a company cannot obtain corporation tax deduction in respect of any shares that are not fully paid up. Having said that, the company can normally deduct an amount equal to the benefit obtained by the employee but only in circumstances where income tax is payable by the employee on that benefit. However, as the arrangement is based on the employee having no income tax liability, any corporation tax deduction that the company may be able to obtain is very limited and based on general principles.

In a group structure, the employee may acquire shares in a company which is not the employer of that employee. The corporation tax deduction can only be claimed by the employer company and not by the company in which the employee acquires shares.

The corporation tax deduction can only be claimed in the accounting period in which shares are allotted to the employee, which, normally, occurs in the accounting period in which shares are acquired and income tax is paid by employees.

*For the employee –*

Like other arrangements such as the JOA and the issue of growth shares by the company, the issue of nil or partly paid shares by a company is more tax efficient than other non-tax efficient option arrangements. Unlike such other arrangements, the nil or partly paid shares arrangement is based on the employee acquiring shares at their full UMV. Whilst employees may pay nothing on acquisition of the nil or partly paid shares, they agree to pay the full UMV of the shares at a future date when called upon by the company whether on demand or on a specified date.

Given that the arrangement is a non-tax advantaged one in terms of any statutory tax reliefs, the employee is not entitled to any tax reliefs on any benefits received under the nil or partly paid shares arrangement. Therefore, the following expected tax implications will arise on the acquisition of nil or partly paid shares in the company.

*Income tax liability?*

The employee will suffer an income tax liability if the employee agrees to acquire nil or partly paid shares for less than the market value of the shares. Any income tax liability is calculated by reference to the difference between the price paid by the employee and the market value of the shares on acquisition.

Income tax will also arise in circumstances where the nil or partly paid shares acquired are restricted securities, if the shares are acquired with an avoidance motive or if the obligation to pay any outstanding amount in the future is written off or otherwise released by the company.

If the employee agrees to pay the full UMV of the nil or partly paid shares, the employee will suffer no general earnings charge to income tax, as there is no discount to the full UMV or undervalue on which to charge income tax. However, the employee will have a liability to income tax by reference to a notional loan to the employee.

To the extent that the employee pays any income tax on any amount representing general earnings of the employee, which takes precedence over the notional loan charge, that amount will be excluded from the notional loan charge.

The notional loan charge applies to securities acquired by reason of employment or for securities that are deemed to be acquired by reason of employment even if the employee does not in fact acquires the shares by reason of his employment with the company but in a different capacity.

For the purpose of the notional loan charge, any amount that the employee agrees to pay in the future is ignored. What counts is what the employee actually pays on acquisition. In the context of the nil or partly paid shares, the employee pays either nothing or a small amount on acquisition so any balance will be included within the notional loan charge if it is not treated as general earnings of the employee.

Essentially, any amount that the employee agrees to pay to the company in the future in respect of the nil or partly paid shares is treated as a notional loan by the company to the employee on which the employee has to pay interest. If interest is not payable by the employee, the amount of the interest is treated as a benefit on which income tax is payable by the employee. This is the notional loan charge. Effectively, income tax charge on the amount of interest that the employee should have paid to the company on the value of the notional loan.

The rate of interest on which income tax is charged is calculated by reference to HMRC's official rate of interest.

The employee will continue to pay the notional loan charge, annually, until the notional loan is discharged or deemed to be discharged by the employee, either on payment of the outstanding amount on the nil or partly paid shares or when the shares are sold in circumstances where the purchaser assumes responsibility for the payment of the outstanding amount to the company.

The death of the employee will also bring the notional loan charge to an end. The notional loan charge also comes to an end when the employee ceases to be employed by the company. However, the notional loan amount may still be charged to income tax if written off by the company but no income tax charge can arise if any chargeable event under the notional loan regime occurs after the period of seven years starting from the date of cessation of employment.

There are certain circumstances under which the employees will not be liable for the notional loan charge. No liability can arise if the notional loan does not exceed the current de minimis amount of £10,000, if tax relief can be obtained by the employee in respect of any commercial loan obtained by the employee in order to acquire shares in the company or where the majority of the nil or partly paid shares, as a class, is not employment related or if that class makes the company employee controlled.

*NICs liability?*

If income tax is due on the acquisition of the nil or partly paid shares as general earnings of the employee and, given that shares that are not fully paid up are always RCAs, the employee's employer will be required to operate the PAYE system and deduct the income tax due from the employee together with the relevant amount representing Class 1 employee's NICs and also account to HMRC for Class 1 employer's NICs. Any income tax is calculated by reference to the best reasonable estimate of the tax liability.

If an income tax liability arises in connection with the notional loan charge, the notional loan charge is treated as a benefit to the employee on which the employer will need to deduct the relevant amount of income tax together with employer's NICs. As the notional loan charge is not general earnings of the employee but a benefit, the deduction will not include an amount in respect of employee's NICs.

*What if the nil or partly paid shares are restricted securities?*

Nil or partly paid shares acquired by employees are likely to be restricted securities and therefore subject to the restricted securities regime.

The arrangement is based on the employee agreeing to pay the full UMV of the shares on acquisition. However, the employee may acquire the shares at a discount by reference to the restricted value or AMV of the shares.

In order to avoid the charge under the restricted securities regime and ensure that any growth in value of the shares is subject to CGT only, the employee needs to opt out of the regime even if the employee agrees to pay the full UMV of the nil or partly paid shares.

The employee will, therefore, need to sign the section 431(1) election, within 14 days of acquisition of the nil or partly paid shares and pay the income tax on the difference between the AMV and the UMV of the shares, if any, so that any benefit received by the employee that represents the difference between the AMV and the UMV is charged to income tax on acquisition of the restricted securities thereby ensuring that any gain on disposal is subject to CGT only.

Otherwise, if the employee agrees to pay an amount which is less than the full UMV of the nil or partly paid shares or if HMRC concludes that any amount agreed to be paid does not reflect the true UMV of the nil or partly paid shares and the employee has not signed the section 431(1) election within the requisite 14 days period, any disposal proceeds received by the employee will be multiplied by a percentage that represents the difference between the AMV and the UMV on acquisition of the nil or partly paid shares and that amount is subject to income tax and, possibly, NICs on disposal of the shares.

Any amount on which income tax is paid in connection with the restricted securities regime is not included in the amount that is treated as a notional loan to the employee.

*On disposal of the nil or partly paid shares?*

When the nil or partly paid shares are ultimately sold or otherwise disposed of by the employee after a period of ownership, CGT may be payable on any gain realised by that employee. CGT is due if the sale proceeds exceed the price that the employee has agreed to pay on acquisition of the nil or partly paid shares. The price that the employee agrees to pay on the acquisition of the nil or partly paid shares is the employee's base cost in the shares.

However, any amount on which income tax is paid by the employee under general earnings, in respect of any discount to the AMV of the nil or partly paid shares, in respect of the opting out of the restricted securities regime or otherwise, is added to the base cost of the nil or partly paid shares. Any income tax charge paid by the employee in connection with the notional loan is not added to the employee's base cost in the shares for CGT purposes.

*Will the employee qualify for ER?*

ER applies to the disposal of ordinary shares in the company. Ordinary shares do not have to include fully paid up shares so, for the purpose of ER, can include nil or partly paid shares.

The employee may, therefore, qualify for ER in respect of the gain provided that the employee can demonstrate compliance with the relevant statutory conditions for the relief in terms of employment and holding of the nil or partly paid shares in the company for at least two years ending with the date of disposal of the shares. In addition, the employee is required to satisfy the requirement for the holding of at least 5% of the ordinary share capital in the company.

It is not unusual for companies who issue nil or partly paid shares to restrict the shares so that the holders have no right to vote. Employees who hold nil or partly paid shares in the company with such restrictions on voting or hold shares that represent less than 5% of the issued share capital of the company will most probably not be entitled to claim the ER in respect of the gain on disposal of the nil or partly paid shares.

## Long Term Incentive Plan (LTIP)

Listed companies invariably rely on the professional services and knowledge of their senior executives. In order to align the financial expectations of shareholders including institutional shareholders of such companies with that of their senior executives, listed companies often wish, and more often are expected, to incentivise their senior executives in the form of share awards. The arrangement can be extended to include other employees of the company but such arrangements are normally limited to senior executives.

An LTIP is a form of long-term incentive arrangement for senior executives of companies listed on the stock exchange or on the Alternative Investment Market (AIM). It is termed 'long-term', as it is normally linked to performance over a period of, typically, three years before senior executives can benefit from any of the awards under the plan. Performance is normally measured by reference to the company's performance.

The LTIP is often operated by listed companies in conjunction with an EBT so that when awards vest on the satisfaction of any performance conditions or when a period of time has elapsed from the date of grant of the awards, shares can be released and delivered to senior executive by the EBT.

The EBT can also be used as a vehicle for the sale of all or some of the shares of senior executives if senior executives wish to sell their shares or are required to convert some of their shares into cash in order to settle any tax liabilities that may arise when shares are issued or transferred to them.

Strictly, an LTIP is not a share or option plan. It is a framework under which a company awards various share or option schemes to its senior executives. The LTIP will normally set out the conditions and other requirements expected from senior executives before any awards can be made under the plan.

Share awards granted under an LTIP are unlikely to be approved or tax-advantaged schemes. This is because either the company is unlikely to comply with the statutory requirements of the approved schemes such as the EMI scheme or the senior executives may not be sufficiently financially incentivised by the CSOP or all-employee schemes, the SAYE scheme and SIP.

The LTIP can include many different types of awards including cash awards. The most common share awards are:

- Nil-cost options – nil cost options are options to receive free shares in the company when all relevant conditions have been satisfied in relation to the award. Being an option, the senior executive can choose the timing of exercise which may occur at any time after the options vest. The senior executive may exercise when the time is right for him or her;

- Conditional share award – this is a very similar award to the nil cost options whereby the executive receives free shares in the company when all relevant conditions have been satisfied in relation to the award. However, the senior executive cannot choose the timing of the award which is made when the conditions are satisfied;

- Restricted shares award – under this award, free shares are awarded to senior executives on the date the award is made and before any of the conditions are satisfied. However, the shares may be forfeited if the conditions are not met by the senior executive. For this reason, the shares are held by an EBT or other trust and only fully released to the senior executive when the conditions are all met;

- Market value options – these are the most common and traditional options whereby senior executives can exercise options to acquire shares in the company at an exercise price which is determined by reference to the market value of the shares on the date of grant. Such market value options will typically be unapproved but can also include the approved CSOP.

The awards can also take the form of phantom options or other arrangements under which the executive is entitled to receive cash as opposed to shares in the company.

Awards made under LTIPs are normally quite generous. They are made on the expectation of growth in the company's value over a period of time which is linked to the performance of the senior executive.

However, financial performance or growth may not be achieved by the company or may later prove to be miscalculated or wrongly determined. For this reason, LTIPs can, in certain specified circumstances, include malus and clawback provisions or other provisions restricting or limiting the vesting of any awards or allowing the forfeiture of shares already awarded.

Malus provisions apply so that any awards can be adjustment downward before the relevant award vests and clawback provisions apply so that any cash award is paid back to the company or shares forfeited where the relevant award has already vested.

Such provisions may apply for a period of two to three years after the performance period but could be for up to 10 years from the date the award is made. They are normally applied in cases of misconduct or poor performance by the senior executive or in other fraudulent circumstances such as when accounts are manipulated to show a false financial strength rather than the company's real financial position.

Senior executives will normally be required to remain in employment for at least three years. Any award which has not already vested may be forfeited if the senior executive is a bad leaver. If a good leaver, the senior executive may keep all of the awards or a proportion of them.

The LTIP may also impose a retention period of two years until a pay-out is made in order to ensure that the senior executive is committed to the company for at least five years.

*Do the shares need to be valued?*

As referred to above, an LTIP may include a number of share awards most of which will be non-tax advantaged schemes. The schemes in the LTIP will, quite likely, award free shares to senior executives as well as options to acquire shares at the exercise price on the date of grant.

The issue or transfer of shares to senior executives will probably give rise to an income tax liability so the value of the shares will need to be determined in order to correctly calculate any such liability that may arise by reference to any benefit received by employees or by reference to the restricted securities regime.

LTIPs are more likely to be set up by listed companies, the market value in which can easily be determined by reference to the published value of the shares at the relevant date. However, LTIPs can also be set up by private companies so valuation of the shares is very important.

Ordinarily, any transaction involving shares in the company, that may give rise to a tax liability, should be valued in any event. Valuation of the shares is not a statutory requirement but is highly recommended. Therefore, a company will need to obtain independent valuation of the shares in the company both the AMV and the UMV when any transaction in shares occurs more specifically between the company and its employees.

Given the unapproved nature of the arrangements, the company is not able to agree valuation with HMRC before unapproved arrangements take place so the company will need to ensure that any such valuation is properly undertaken. To avoid any liability to income tax or to keep any such liability to a minimum, the value of the shares will need to be as accurate as possible.

*Do the arrangements need to be notified?*

The company must notify HMRC when it issues employment related securities to its employees. The notification must be done online through the ERS online filing system and, in respect of the first registration and notification, the company must make the notification by the 6 July following the end of the tax year in which a reportable event occurs during that tax year. The scheme can still be registered and notified to HMRC by the 6 July following the end of the tax year in which it is implemented.

The company must register all non-tax advantaged share option schemes with HMRC. It may do so separately in respect of each non-tax advantaged scheme or register all of them under the same registration number. If all non-tax advantaged share schemes are registered under the same registration number, the company will need to file one annual return. Otherwise, the company will need to file an annual return in respect of each of the non-tax advantaged schemes.

The company is also required to complete online annual returns. All annual returns must be submitted by 6 July after the end of the relevant tax year. The company must notify any changes that may affect the holding of shares in the company.

The company must complete the annual return even if there have been no changes that require notification.

Tax treatment of LTIPs

*For the Company –*

The company will, normally, be entitled to a statutory corporation tax deduction in connection with non-tax advantaged share or option schemes. The company can deduct an amount equal to the benefit obtained by the employee when the options are exercised or otherwise when shares are issued or transferred to the employee. This is the most valuable deduction the company can get in connection with the scheme.

However, if the company wishes to obtain a deduction for the amounts spent on setting up the scheme and the operation of the scheme throughout its life or in respect of any benefit received by employees which is not subject to a statutory corporation tax deduction, the company may need to rely on general principles of corporation tax deduction.

In a group structure, the employee may receive shares or otherwise exercise options to acquire shares in a company which is not the employer of that employee. The corporation tax deduction can only be claimed by the employer company and not by the company in which the employee acquires shares.

The corporation tax deduction can only be claimed in the accounting period in which shares are allotted or transferred to the employee, which, normally, occurs in the accounting period when the shares or other benefit is received by the employee or exercise of the options takes place.

*For the employee –*

As the LTIP itself is not a share or option scheme, the tax implications will need to be considered by reference to each award under the LTIP. Given that, in the context of listed companies, most awards under the LTIP are unapproved or non-tax advantaged, the employee will not be entitled to any tax reliefs on any benefits received under the schemes.

To the extent any of the schemes are approved or tax-advantaged, statutory tax reliefs may be available as described in relation to the particular approved scheme.

*On the date of grant?*

To the extent an award under the LTIP includes an option to acquire shares in the company, the grant of options will not normally give rise to any tax implications when options are granted to employees.

*Income tax liability?*

When options are exercised by the employee or when shares are issued or transferred to an employee pursuant to an award of shares or where the award is the payment of cash to the employee, income tax will normally be payable on the difference between the AMV of the shares acquired and the exercise price actually paid by the employee. If the employee pays nothing for the shares, the whole value is subject to income tax.

If the award is in respect of any of the approved share or option schemes, the income tax liability will be calculated as referred to in respect of the relevant scheme.

*NICs liability?*

If, at the time of exercise of the options or when shares are issued or transferred to an employee pursuant to an award of shares, the shares are RCAs or where the award is the payment of cash to the employee, the employee's employer will be required to operate the PAYE system and deduct the income tax due from the employee together with the relevant amount representing Class 1 employee's NICs and also account to HMRC for Class 1 employer's NICs.

The shares of listed companies or companies listed on AIM are always RCAs. For this reason, the NICs liability of the employer and the obligation to operate the PAYE system will always apply to those shares.

If an income tax liability arises in connection with the exercise of the shares in circumstances where the employer company is required to operate the PAYE system and deduct the amount of income tax from the employee together with primary Class 1 NICs. The employer will need to pay to HMRC the amount deducted together with the secondary Class 1 NICs.

However, in certain circumstances, the employer may recover its liability in respect of the secondary Class 1 NICs from the employee. It can do so either by way of recovery from the employee or by transferring it to the employee.

*What if the shares are restricted securities?*

Shares acquired by employees following an exercise of options awarded under an unapproved share option scheme or when shares are issued or transferred to an employee pursuant to an award of shares, are very likely to be restricted securities and therefore subject to the restricted securities regime.

In order to avoid the charge under the restricted securities regime, the employee needs to consider signing the section 4311() election?

The employee acquiring restricted securities may wish to consider the implications of the restricted securities regime. The employee will have two options:

- Sign the section 431(1) election within 14 days of acquisition so that any benefit received by the employee that represents the difference between the AMV and the UMV is charged to income tax and is payable on acquisition of the restricted securities. In which case any gain on disposal is subject to CGT only; or

- Not sign the election but then any disposal proceeds are multiplied by a percentage that represents the difference between the AMV and the UMV on acquisition and that amount is subject to income tax and possibly NICs on disposal of the shares.

There is no equivalent deeming provision in respect of the acquisition of restricted securities following exercise of options under an unapproved share option scheme or when shares are issued or transferred to an employee pursuant to a reward of shares under a non-tax advantaged scheme, as is the case with approved option schemes. Therefore, the employee will need to consider signing the election in any event. The company may require employees to sign the section 431(1) election on exercise or acquisition of shares.

When restricted shares are acquired in respect of any of the approved schemes, the employee does not need to consider the two options above, as the legislation provides a deeming provision in connection with the section 431(1) election. So effectively, the employee is deemed to have signed the election and, as a consequence, any gain on disposal of the restricted shares will only be subject to CGT.

However, the legislation also provides that the deeming provision falls away if income tax is payable in respect of any of the approved schemes. The obvious solution is, therefore, for the employee to sign the election, in any event, even if the company and the employee are not aware of any issues that may give rise to an income tax liability in connection with any of the approved schemes.

*On disposal of the shares?*

When any shares are ultimately sold or otherwise disposed of by the employee, either immediately following exercise of an option, acquisition of shares or after a period of ownership, CGT may be payable on any gain realised by that shareholder.

CGT is due if the sale proceeds exceed the price that the employee paid on exercise of the options or when they are acquired. The price paid by the employee on exercise or on acquisition is the employee's base cost in the shares. However, any amount on which income tax is paid by the employee together with any liability of the employer to Class 1 NICs that is transferred to the employee is added to the base cost of the shares.

If shares, acquired under an unapproved share option scheme, are disposed of by the employee immediately after acquisition, CGT is not likely to arise, as the liability of the employee to income tax on any benefit will result in the base cost in the shares being equal to the market value of the shares on disposal.

*Will the employee qualify for ER?*

The employee may qualify for ER in respect of the gain provided that the employee can demonstrate compliance with the relevant statutory conditions for the relief in terms of employment and holding of shares in the company for at least two years ending with the date of disposal of the shares.

In addition, the employee will need to satisfy the requirement for the holding of at least 5% of the ordinary share capital in the company. Therefore, if an employee holds shares that represent less than 5% of the ordinary share capital of the company, the employee will not be entitled to claim the ER.

# CHAPTER ELEVEN
# CONCLUSION

As we have seen, both private and listed companies are able to offer share awards to their employees. Some are eligible to grant options to their employees to acquire shares in the future or award shares immediately under approved arrangements with the benefit of statutory tax reliefs for both the relevant company and the employees.

Companies that are not able to set up and operate approved schemes can always consider any of the numerous unapproved schemes that are available to both private and listed companies. Indeed, companies can also consider the unapproved schemes even in circumstances where other approved schemes are available to them. They may wish to do so where additional awards are required beyond the ones already awarded under the approved schemes.

Care must be taken to ensure that a detailed analysis is undertaken by companies in order to establish in advance that they are able to set up and operate a particular scheme for the benefit of its employees. All relevant statutory provisions and regulations together with any listing rules must be considered in order to ensure compliance for a valid scheme.

The information provided herein in relation to the approved schemes and some of the unapproved ones is not sufficiently detailed but provide a very good overview of the schemes that are available to companies together with the general tax implications that may result to both the company and its employees on acquisition of shares or exercise of any options to acquire shares in the company or other member of the company's group.

HMRC's latest report on share schemes shows that the EMI scheme is the most popular approved scheme among small and medium sized businesses. The other three approved schemes, CSOP, SAYE and SIP, only make up 17% of all approved schemes. The EMI scheme's popularity is quite obvious given its flexibility together with the generous tax benefits that are available for both the employer company and its employees.

The income tax and NICs savings for employees under all four approved schemes nearly totalled £1 billion in 2017/18. This is slightly lower than previous years but mainly due to the other three approved schemes becoming less and less popular with companies. However, businesses should still consider the benefits of the other three schemes, the CSOP in particular, that can be used in addition to an EMI scheme or where companies are not able to meet the requirements or any of them under the EMI legislation.

It is very clear from the report that the use of share schemes by businesses benefits not only companies and their employees but also the UK economy as a whole. The government is therefore willing to continue to offer generous tax benefits to both companies and employees so, whilst EMI schemes are extensively used by companies, other approved schemes should be considered by companies as a viable investment and a form of incentive and encouragement to their employees so that they are not abandoned for lack of interest.

As regards Brexit, the UK's departure from the EU may have an impact on the above schemes, more particularly the approved ones. The impact may not be so great though but it is important to keep an eye on any future developments in connection with both approved and unapproved schemes.

Given the fact that share and option schemes, whether approved or unapproved, benefit and contribute to the UK economy, it is very likely that the government will want to make sure that any tax reliefs are preserved going forward and that UK companies remain competitive and continue to incentivise and encourage their employees to take a stake in the company so that employees feel sufficiently rewarded and consequently assist and be part of any future growth and success of the company.

# MORE BOOKS BY LAW BRIEF PUBLISHING

A selection of our other titles available now:-

| |
|---|
| 'Ellis on Credit Hire – Sixth Edition' by Aidan Ellis & Tim Kevan |
| 'Tackling Disclosure in the Criminal Courts – A Practitioner's Guide' by Narita Bahra QC & Don Ramble |
| 'A Practical Guide to TOLATA Claims' by Greg Williams |
| 'Artificial Intelligence – The Practical Legal Issues' by John Buyers |
| 'A Practical Guide to Prison Injury Claims' by Malcolm Johnson |
| 'A Practical Guide to Hackney Carriage Licensing in London' by Stuart Jessop |
| 'A Practical Guide to Advising Clients at the Police Station' by Colin Stephen McKeown-Beaumont |
| 'A Practical Guide to Antisocial Behaviour Injunctions' by Iain Wightwick |
| 'Practical Mediation: A Guide for Mediators, Advocates, Advisers, Lawyers, and Students in Civil, Commercial, Business, Property, Workplace, and Employment Cases' by Jonathan Dingle with John Sephton |
| 'Planning Obligations Demystified: A Practical Guide to Planning Obligations and Section 106 Agreements' by Bob Mc Geady & Meyric Lewis |
| 'A Practical Guide to Crofting Law' by Brian Inkster |
| 'A Practical Guide to Spousal Maintenance' by Liz Cowell |
| 'A Practical Guide to the Law of Domain Names and Cybersquatting' by Andrew Clemson |
| 'A Practical Guide to the Law of Gender Pay Gap Reporting' by Harini Iyengar |
| 'A Practical Guide to the Rights of Grandparents in Children Proceedings' by Stuart Barlow |
| 'NHS Whistleblowing and the Law' by Joseph England |
| 'Employment Law and the Gig Economy' by Nigel Mackay & Annie Powell |
| 'A Practical Guide to the General Data Protection Regulation (GDPR)' by Keith Markham |

'A Practical Guide to Noise Induced Hearing Loss (NIHL) Claims' by Andrew Mckie, Ian Skeate, Gareth McAloon

'An Introduction to Beauty Negligence Claims – A Practical Guide for the Personal Injury Practitioner' by Greg Almond

'Intercompany Agreements for Transfer Pricing Compliance' by Paul Sutton

'Zen and the Art of Mediation' by Martin Plowman

'A Practical Guide to the SRA Principles, Individual and Law Firm Codes of Conduct 2019 – What Every Law Firm Needs to Know' by Paul Bennett

'A Practical Guide to Licensing Law for Commercial Property Lawyers' by Niall McCann & Richard Williams

'A Practical Guide to Adoption for Family Lawyers' by Graham Pegg

'Essential Motor Finance Law for the Busy Practitioner' by Richard Humphreys

'A Practical Guide to Industrial Disease Claims' by Andrew Mckie & Ian Skeate

'A Practical Guide to the Law of Armed Conflict' by Jo Morris & Libby Anderson

'A Practical Guide to Redundancy' by Philip Hyland

'A Practical Guide to Vicarious Liability' by Mariel Irvine

'A Practical Guide to Claims Arising from Delays in Diagnosing Cancer' by Bella Webb

'A Practical Guide to Applications for Landlord's Consent and Variation of Leases' by Mark Shelton

'A Practical Guide to Relief from Sanctions Post-Mitchell and Denton' by Peter Causton

'Butler's Equine Tax Planning: 2nd Edition' by Julie Butler

'A Practical Guide to Equity Release for Advisors' by Paul Sams

'A Practical Guide to Unlawful Eviction and Harassment' by Stephanie Lovegrove

'A Practical Guide to the Law Relating to Food' by Ian Thomas

'A Practical Guide to the Ending of Assured Shorthold Tenancies' by Elizabeth Dwomoh

'A Practical Guide to Financial Services Claims' by Chris Hegarty

'The Law of Houses in Multiple Occupation: A Practical Guide to HMO Proceedings' by Julian Hunt

'A Practical Guide to Unlawful Eviction and Harassment' by Stephanie Lovegrove

| |
|---|
| 'A Practical Guide to Solicitor and Client Costs' by Robin Dunne |
| 'A Practical Guide to Wrongful Conception, Wrongful Birth and Wrongful Life Claims' by Rebecca Greenstreet |
| 'Occupiers, Highways and Defective Premises Claims: A Practical Guide Post-Jackson – 2nd Edition' by Andrew Mckie |
| 'A Practical Guide to Financial Ombudsman Service Claims' by Adam Temple & Robert Scrivenor |
| 'A Practical Guide to the Law of Enfranchisement and Lease Extension' by Paul Sams |
| 'A Practical Guide to Marketing for Lawyers – 2nd Edition' by Catherine Bailey & Jennet Ingram |
| 'A Practical Guide to Advising Schools on Employment Law' by Jonathan Holden |
| 'Certificates of Lawful Use and Development: A Guide to Making and Determining Applications' by Bob Mc Geady & Meyric Lewis |
| 'A Practical Guide to the Law of Dilapidations' by Mark Shelton |
| 'A Guide to Consent in Clinical Negligence Post-Montgomery' by Lauren Sutherland QC |
| 'A Practical Guide to Running Housing Disrepair and Cavity Wall Claims: 2nd Edition' by Andrew Mckie & Ian Skeate |
| 'A Practical Guide to Digital and Social Media Law for Lawyers' by Sherree Westell |
| 'A Practical Guide to Holiday Sickness Claims – 2nd Edition' by Andrew Mckie & Ian Skeate |
| 'A Practical Guide to Elderly Law' by Justin Patten |
| 'Arguments and Tactics for Personal Injury and Clinical Negligence Claims' by Dorian Williams |
| 'A Practical Guide to QOCS and Fundamental Dishonesty' by James Bentley |
| 'A Practical Guide to Drone Law' by Rufus Ballaster, Andrew Firman, Eleanor Clot |
| 'A Practical Guide to Compliance for Personal Injury Firms Working With Claims Management Companies' by Paul Bennett |
| 'A Practical Guide to the Landlord and Tenant Act 1954: Commercial Tenancies' by Richard Hayes & David Sawtell |
| 'A Practical Guide to Psychiatric Claims in Personal Injury' by Liam Ryan |
| 'A Practical Guide to Dog Law for Owners and Others' by Andrea Pitt |

| |
|---|
| 'RTA Allegations of Fraud in a Post-Jackson Era: The Handbook – 2nd Edition' by Andrew Mckie |
| 'RTA Personal Injury Claims: A Practical Guide Post-Jackson' by Andrew Mckie |
| 'On Experts: CPR35 for Lawyers and Experts' by David Boyle |
| 'An Introduction to Personal Injury Law' by David Boyle |
| 'A Practical Guide to Claims Arising From Accidents Abroad and Travel Claims' by Andrew Mckie & Ian Skeate |
| 'A Practical Guide to Chronic Pain Claims' by Pankaj Madan |
| 'A Practical Guide to Claims Arising from Fatal Accidents' by James Patience |
| 'A Practical Approach to Clinical Negligence Post-Jackson' by Geoffrey Simpson-Scott |
| 'Employers' Liability Claims: A Practical Guide Post-Jackson' by Andrew Mckie |
| 'A Practical Guide to Subtle Brain Injury Claims' by Pankaj Madan |
| 'A Practical Guide to Costs in Personal Injury Cases' by Matthew Hoe |
| 'The No Nonsense Solicitors' Practice: A Guide To Running Your Firm' by Bettina Brueggemann |
| 'The Queen's Counsel Lawyer's Omnibus: 20 Years of Cartoons from The Times 1993-2013' by Alex Steuart Williams |

These books and more are available to order online direct from the publisher at www.lawbriefpublishing.com, where you can also read free sample chapters. For any queries, contact us on 0844 587 2383 or mail@lawbriefpublishing.com.

Our books are also usually in stock at www.amazon.co.uk with free next day delivery for Prime members, and at good legal bookshops such as Wildy & Sons.

We are regularly launching new books in our series of practical day-to-day practitioners' guides. Visit our website and join our free newsletter to be kept informed and to receive special offers, free chapters, etc.

You can also follow us on Twitter at www.twitter.com/lawbriefpub.

www.ingramcontent.com/pod-product-compliance
Lightning Source LLC
LaVergne TN
LVHW052327200926
848481LV00002B/691

* 9 7 8 1 9 1 2 6 8 7 4 6 6 *